Empowering Native American Stories For Children

Embarking on Empowering Journeys of Resilience, Wisdom, and Cultural Pride to Enrich Young Hearts and Minds

Welcome Aboard, Check Out This Limited-Time Free Bonus!

Ahoy, reader! Welcome to the Ahoy Publications family, and thanks for snagging a copy of this book! Since you've chosen to join us on this journey, we'd like to offer you something special.

Check out the link below for a FREE e-book filled with delightful facts about American History.

But that's not all - you'll also have access to our exclusive email list with even more free e-books and insider knowledge. Well, what are ye waiting for? Click the link below to join and set sail toward exciting adventures in American History.

Access your bonus here

https://ahoypublications.com/

Or, Scan the QR code!

Table of Contents

Introduction

It's common to talk about Native Americans as if they're all the same, no matter where they're from. However, every tribe has its own unique identity, with a rich history, culture, traditions, beliefs, and legends. There are many interesting tales and facts about each Native American tribe that show their similarities and their differences. This book is a great way for kids to learn about how they lived through a collection of stories and myths. Pictures and maps help you get a better idea of the information provided, and the topics are presented in a way that makes them easy to understand.

There is a lot that you can learn from the Native Americans. Still, many schools from other cultures mostly focus on history from a European point of view. They talk about the wars and only touch on the horrible treatment given to the tribes during the relocation to reservations. Yet there is so much more to them than their conflict with the colonists and settlers. Every tribe has a way of life that developed long before anyone sailed across the ocean and set foot on their shores. The culture of every tribe is unique, and they can give you a new way of looking at the world.

While this book is meant to be educational, it's not some boring textbook. There are snippets of information to help you understand the basics of each tribe. Then, it dives into stories that go deeper into the experiences of people who lived through the days when the continent was just for them. These tales are fun and exciting, and they'll make you think about using their lessons in your life. If you enjoy learning new things, this book will give you plenty of stories and facts you've never heard!

Chapter 1: The Navajo Way

The Navajo are a major Native American tribe from the Southwestern United States. They have the biggest reservation in the country, which stretches across the Four Corners. This region includes the states of Utah, Arizona, New Mexico, and Colorado. The Navajo people have a rich storytelling tradition, passing down tales of their tribe's mythology from generation to generation. Their artwork also tells stories, using pictures and symbols to represent major figures or events from their history and religion.

Flag of the Navajo Nation[1]

Hogans

Hogans are the type of home that the Navajo people live in. They can be built in shapes like cones, squares, rounded tops, or have multiple sides. The walls are made from packed earth, stone, and timber, while the roofs are created using tree bark. By packing mud onto the walls of their hogans, the Navajo were able to insulate and protect their homes from the summer heat, and it also kept their hogans warm in the cold winter months. Many Navajo still live in hogans, as these dwellings are considered very energy efficient, making it easy to stay comfortable without needing things like air conditioners or heaters.

Navajo Winter Hogan.[2]

Important Symbols of the Navajo Tribe

Sun: This symbol represents everything in the universe being in harmony. All living things need the sun to survive, and all living things are at their best when they work together. The sun also brings good luck, happiness, and plentiful harvests.

Water: This symbol represents life and balance. Like the sun, all living things need water to survive, but while the sun brings life from the outside, water gives life from the inside. It also shows how nothing is permanent. Just like how the course of a river can change over time, life also continues to change.

Lightning: This symbol represents speed and agility. Lightning streaks all across the sky in a single instant, often moving faster than sound. It can also be a warning against doing things that could bring bad luck.

Bear: This symbol represents strength, endurance, and durability. The bear is a very powerful animal, being large and imposing. When you see a bear, it is a sign to accept your past in order to overcome obstacles and have a successful future. It is also a warning to prepare and build up defenses against danger.

Thunderbird: This symbol represents a sudden rush of happiness. As a mythological creature, the thunderbird is believed to only appear when the blessings given to the tribe are plentiful. It can also be seen as a sign of peace and serenity for those who see the great creature.

Arrow: This symbol represents protection and safety. Bows and arrows were one of the main weapons used by the Navajo people to hunt and fight, so the arrow is considered something that helps to keep them safe from predators and enemies. It also serves as a warning to anyone who might seek to harm them that they are willing to use violence to protect themselves and their people.

The Coyote

The Coyote is a trickster god in Navajo mythology with power over the rain. He is an important figure in many of the stories the Navajo people tell, always creating mischief and causing problems for those he meets. The Coyote won his wife, Changing Bear, by cheating in a contest and using his magic to make her evil. Like the Coyote, Changing Bear was able to transform from a human into an animal form. Together, they became a dangerous couple, always looking for new ways to cause trouble. Nobody knows why the Coyote enjoys being nasty and tricking people like that. Still, whenever he turns up, anyone he meets must be careful not to become his next victim.

Changing Bear and Her Brothers

After the Coyote taught Changing Bear how to use the innate power of water to find out the location of her brothers, she turned into a human and went to meet them. She flattered them by complimenting their hair and reminded them how she used to comb it for them to check for lice.

The brothers of Changing Bear didn't want their hair to become filled with lice, so they agreed to let her comb it for them like she did before the Coyote made her evil. They trusted their sister and turned their backs on her. She transformed into a she-bear, mauling them to death while the Coyote howled in laughter.

The Coyote and the Giant

Sometimes, the Coyote's mischief can be helpful, even though that's not his intention.

There was a giant who was terrorizing the land, destroying villages, and eating the people he found there, including their small children. One day, the Coyote raced past the giant, and the giant ran after him. However, the giant was too slow and couldn't catch up. The Coyote returned to the giant and convinced the monster that he could make it so the giant could run as fast as him. The giant agreed, and the Coyote broke his leg and then spit on it, telling the giant that this would heal it and strengthen the bones and muscles. This turned out to be a trick, and the giant now had trouble walking, unable to catch up to the smallest of children as they ran away from him!

The Yéii

The Yéii are benevolent or good divine spirits that help the Navajo people. While there are many different types of Yéii, the ones most honored are the Holy People (Diyin Diné'e). They are connected to the forces of nature and were among the first beings who eventually helped create our world. The Yéii have power over things like rain, wind, earth, plants, and fire. When the time came to settle down, they shaped the world around them, creating things in nature that let people survive. It's considered a good idea to offer thanks and blessings to the Yéii, as they can use their powers to help bring good fortune to the Navajo people.

Diné Bahane' (Story of the People)

The Diné Bahane' is the Navajo people's story about the creation of the universe. It tells the tale of how there were originally four worlds, each bringing something different into being. The fourth and final world was the one where regular humans came from. There were also the Yéii, divine spirits known as the Holy People, who helped to shape the world as it's known today. The First Man and First Woman journeyed across the four worlds to explore the creatures and environments that came into existence.

The Dark World (First World)

In the beginning, the Dark World (Ni' Hodiłhił) was a chaotic and unruly place. The four seas stretched as far as the eye could see, and floating at their center was a small island. Many beings lived in the Dark World. The first and foremost were the Diyin Dine'é, also known as the Holy People. They were powerful supernatural spirits who used their magic to shape the land and bring knowledge to others. Also living in the Dark World were the Coyote, the Four Rulers of the Seas, Beings of the Mists, the Insect People, and the Bat People. The Bat People were considered Air-Spirit People, using their massive wings to control the skies.

When the First Man and the First Woman came into being, they lived on separate ends of the island. Both of them built large fires to help them stay warm at night. Upon seeing each other's fires from across the island, they set out to find whoever had made the fire. After walking for days, the First Man and Woman met at the island's center and realized they were meant to be together. They fell in love, deciding to live as husband and wife. The pair were happy to have found one another and for a while, everything seemed to be perfect. They used great power to create the Holy People, who banded together to form the First Tribe.

However, their happiness would not last, as the Dark World was a violent place. All the different beings were constantly at war with one another, but the First Man and Woman wanted to live in peace. They were able to get wings from the Air-Spirit People, which allowed them and their tribe to explore far across the seas in the hope that they could find a new land where they would be able to live in harmony with everything around them. After searching for days, they failed to find any new lands but instead discovered an opening in the sky that was a great distance away in the East. The tribe flew through the opening, chancing that whatever they may find would be better than the Dark World.

The Blue World (Second World)

After flying through the opening in the East of the Dark World, the First Man and Woman led their tribe as they entered the Blue World (Ni' Hodootł'izh). They found that nearly all the creatures living there were colored blue. There were blue-feathered birds and blue-furred animals, and the blue swallows were the main inhabitants of the Blue World. The blue swallows' ruler, Chief Swallow, was offended when he saw the Holy People enter his domain from the Dark World. He confronted them and demanded that they leave at once.

Although the First Man and Woman liked the Blue World, they knew they couldn't stay. The Swallow Chief threatened to attack the pair, and they didn't want to fight. The First Man uncovered a deposit of beautiful black gemstones known as jet, and he used these gemstones with wood from the trees of the Blue World to create a magical wand. With his new wand, the First Man made a wish that their tribe could walk into the sky, where there was another opening far to the South. They left the Blue World together, leaving the Chief Swallow and the other creatures behind, hoping the next place they found could be their new home.

The Yellow World (Third World)

When the Holy People emerged from the opening, they saw they were in the Yellow World (Ni' Haltsooí). It was a wondrous place, with rushing rivers and towering mountains dominating the landscape. Like the other worlds, the Yellow World was filled with many strange and interesting creatures, yet there was no sun in the sky, so everything was covered in darkness. The Holy People followed the rivers and stopped at the spot where two rivers came together to form a cross. Behind them, the Sacred Mountains stretched so high the tribe couldn't even see their peaks. It seemed like a good place to live, as the creatures weren't at war and didn't try to drive them out.

Unfortunately, the Coyote from the Dark World had followed the Holy People, looking for new ways to create mischief. There was a monster in the Yellow World known as Tééhooltsódii, or the Big Water Creature. The Coyote stole her children, and in her anger, she unleashed a great flood. Since the Holy People lived at the point where the rivers converged, the great flood came and washed away their settlement. Everything they had built was destroyed. Knowing they couldn't stay in the Yellow World any longer, the First Man and Woman searched the lands until they found an opening in the West. They took their tribe and left through an opening, uncertain if fate would be kinder in the next world.

The White World (Fourth World)

The Holy People traveled through the opening and came out the other side into the White World (Ni' Hodisxǫs). In this world, the magic of the Holy People was even more powerful than before. They built a new settlement on the banks of a great river but were careful not to place their homes too close to the water. The First Man had taken some soil from the Yellow World, and with his wand, he used it to recreate the Sacred Mountains in the White World. The Holy People then created the Sun, Moon, Stars, and even the Seasons.

The Coyote followed the Holy People again and went to the tribe's settlement to create more mischief. He threw a stone in the river and declared that if the stone sank, anyone who died would be sent back to the previous worlds. As soon as the stone hit the water, it dropped to the bottom of the river, and the Coyote told the Holy People that he had created Death. This upset the tribe, but there were no more worlds where they could go, so they had no choice but to accept that Death was now a part of their reality.

The First Man and Woman gave birth to a child named the White Shell Woman (Yoołgaii Asdzą́ą́). When she grew up, she became known as the Changing Woman (Asdzą́ą́ Nádleehé), and fell in love with the Sun. The Changing Woman gave birth to the Hero Twins, a pair of beings named Monster Slayer (Naayéé' Neizghání) and Born For Water (Tóbájíshchíní). The Hero Twins went on many adventures across the White World, where they encountered the Anaye, a group of evil monsters that lived in the dark places untouched by their father, the Sun. The Hero Twins spent many Seasons battling the monsters, eventually ridding the world of the Anaye.

After coming to the White World, the Holy People had children who were all human beings. Unlike their parents, the humans had no powers but were inventive and had strong inner spirits. They created tools, weapons, and new shelters that kept them safe from the outside world. The humans explored the lands and came together to form new tribes. However, they never forgot where they came from and honored their ancestors through sacred rituals and ceremonies. The modern tribes still practice many of these rituals and ceremonies, keeping the spirit of the Holy People alive.

Chapter Round-Up Activity

Can you tell what someone is trying to tell you when they only use a simple picture to communicate? The Navajo have many symbols that help them express different ideas about the world around them. See if you can match these symbols to their meanings:

Bear

Peace and Serenity

Sun

Ruler of the Blue World

Water

Good Luck and Happiness

Lightning

Trickster God

Thunderbird

Evil Monster

Wand

Safety and Protection

Anaye

Strength, Endurance, and
Durability

Chief Swallow

Speed and Agility

Arrow

Made With Jet

Coyote

Life and Balance

Chapter 2: Lakota Legends: The Buffalo and the Sioux

The Lakota tribe are members of the Sioux Nation. They are one of the three main tribes that make up the Sioux. Nowadays, they mostly live in North and South Dakota. However, the Sioux were originally spread across much of the Midwest of the United States, including the Great Plains region. Like all members of the Sioux Nation, the Lakota speak the Siouan language, but their dialect is known as Lakȟótiyapi. Around 1730, the Cheyenne people introduced the Lakota to horses, which became a major part of the Sioux culture.

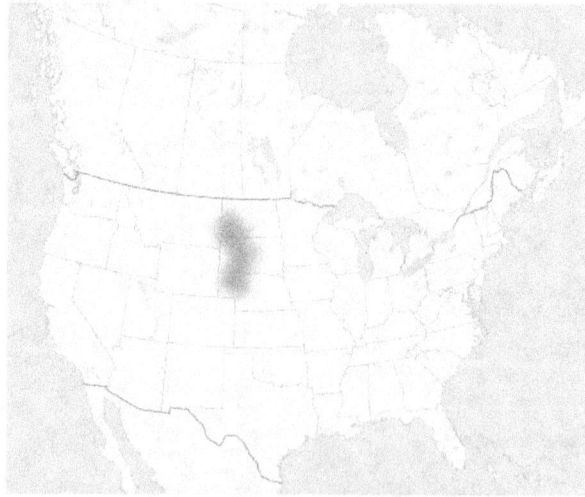

The Map of Lakota.[8]

Lakota Subtribes

There are seven subtribes of the Lakota. Their names are in the Lakota language, but they have English translations that many non-Native Americans know them by. The seven subtribes of the Lakota include:

Blackfoot/Blackfeet (Sihásapa): The Blackfoot subtribe of the Lakota has a name similar to the Blackfoot Confederacy, which lives in the Great Plains part of the United States. Still, they are entirely separate from one another. The Lakota Blackfeet dwelled in the western portion of North and South Dakota, but they now live on the Standing Rock Reservation, which stretches across both North and South Dakota, and the Cheyenne River Reservation in South Dakota, where they share the land with other subtribes of the Lakota.

Brulé/Burnt Thighs (Sičháŋǧu): They mainly lived on the Rosebud Indian Reservation in the southwestern portion of South Dakota, but smaller groups of the Brulé subtribe have settled on the Lower Brule Indian Reservation in central South Dakota along the western bank of the Missouri River. There are also some members of the Brulé on the Pine Ridge Indian Reservation, located to the west of the Rosebud Indian Reservation. Bob Barker, the former longtime host of the CBS game show *The Price Is Right*, was a member of the Brulé, and spent much of his youth on the Rosebud Indian Reservation.

Miniconjou/Plants by the Water (Mnikȟówožu): They once lived in the western portion of South Dakota, from the Black Hills to the Platte River. Currently, they inhabit the west-central part of the state. They were called "Plants by the Water" because the Miniconjou built settlements near rivers and grew their crops nearby. The Two Kettles subtribe was originally part of the Miniconjou but split off in 1840 to form their own subtribe. The Miniconjou's most famous chief was Touch the Clouds, who was revered as a great warrior and diplomat.

Sans Arc/Without Bows (Itázipčho): While their name "Sans Arc" is French for "Without Bows," their true name means "no markings." Their name refers to the fact that the Sans Arc hunters never put markings on their arrows. Most tribes would mark their arrows to prove who killed the prey they hunted, especially buffalo or bison. However, the Sans Arc people left their arrows unmarked so that everyone could share the meat they received from their kills. This generosity was well-known within the Lakota tribe, and the tale of the White Buffalo

Woman claimed it was due to this trait that she gave the peace pipe to the Sans Arc people.

Hunkpapa/Head of the Circle (Húŋkpapȟa): Along with several other Lakota subtribes, they were among the first Native American tribes to fight alongside the United States during the American Indian Wars. The Hunkpapa got their name because they built their lodges at the entrance to the Great Council circle, where all the members of the Sioux Nation would meet. Sitting Bull, a famous Lakota leader who fought in the Battle of Little Bighorn against the United States Army's 7th Cavalry Regiment under the command of Lieutenant Colonel George Armstrong Custer, was a member of the Hunkpapa.

Two Kettles/Two Boilings (Oóhenuŋpa): They are considered members of the Central Lakota and currently live on the Cheyenne River Indian Reservation. During the 19th century, they lived in smaller groups along the Missouri and Cheyenne Rivers, migrating with the herds of buffalo or bison. The Two Kettles people had a mostly peaceful relationship with the European settlers, engaging in trade and welcoming them as guests. Unlike some other subtribes of the Lakota, they were willing to sign peace treaties, promising not to attack the settlers unless it was in self-defense.

Oglala/They Scatter Their Own (Oglála): They began trading beaver and bison furs with the European settlers who came out west during the early 19th century. However, tensions between the settlers and Native Americans increased – especially after the Sioux signed the Fort Laramie Treaty with the United States federal government in 1868. After that, the Oglala resisted any attempt to force them onto a reservation. Ultimately, they had no choice but to submit; they now live on the Pine Ridge Indian Reservation in South Dakota. Crazy Horse was a leader of the Oglala and a hero to his people for his actions during the Battle of Little Bighorn.

The Chief and the Buffalo

The flickering flame from a single candle cast a soft orange light over a piece of paper lying on the small table. The Lakota Chief sat beside the table and stared at the treaty he was supposed to sign . . . to agree with his tribe moving from their ancestral lands to a reservation. The man from the government promised the Chief that they would be very comfortable and have the entire reservation to themselves, allowing them to do whatever they wanted within its borders. But White Men had promised his people many things over the years, and those promises were rarely kept.

Chief Sitting Bull.'

As the hours ticked away, the Chief remained undecided about signing the treaty. Most of the neighboring tribes had already left for the reservations, and his tribe was far too small to put up a fight by themselves. If they tried, they would be killed for certain. Yet the idea of dooming his people to live in what was basically an outdoor prison didn't seem like a much better fate. He was frustrated that he was being forced to choose between two terrible options. Should he sign his name on the treaty, he would forever be remembered as the chief who surrendered.

Glancing out the opening of his teepee, the Chief saw that the moon was full, and the stars were shining brightly, blanketing the lands in a silvery glow. A cool breeze was drifting through the air, fighting off the overbearing summer heat. He decided to go for a walk to clear his head since he wasn't making any progress, just sitting there in his home. Emerging from his teepee, the Chief strolled through his village, wondering how his people would see him if he agreed to the treaty's terms. Would they spit at him, calling him a coward and a traitor? What if he refused to sign it? Would they use their final breath to curse his name as they died for a lost cause? It was an impossible situation.

When the Chief reached the edge of the village, he greeted the tribesman standing guard. There was no sign of trouble beyond the village, so the Chief headed off into the plains alone and unarmed. He walked for a long while before reaching the river bank, and he wanted to dip his toes in the water while having a quick rest. The Chief sat on the river's edge, letting the rushing river wash over his sore feet, still thinking about his big decision. The sound of footsteps behind him caused him to leap up and whirl around. Even though he wasn't carrying a weapon, he was ready to fight to the death with his hands.

"Do not be alarmed," a voice said.

The Chief wasn't alarmed anymore – now he was in awe. The Great White Buffalo stood before him, towering over the Chief and staring down at him with two huge black eyes. When the Buffalo spoke, his mouth didn't move, and no sounds came from him. Instead, the Chief heard the Buffalo's voice speaking within his mind.

"I know who you are, and I am not scared," he told the Buffalo. "But my heart is heavy tonight. I must make a big decision, and I do not know what to do."

"You wear your burdens like a cloak, Little Chief. I can tell your soul is troubled. I understand why you struggle to make your decision. You feel there is little difference between confinement on a reservation and certain death in a fight."

"That is true, oh Great One," the Chief replied. "Please, tell me which I should choose."

"I cannot tell you that," the Buffalo said. "This is something you must decide for yourself. Look deep in your heart and listen to what it tells you."

"My heart was broken long ago, when my people were scattered and forced to survive apart from one another. It has been silent for many years."

"Your heart is like your people," the Buffalo stated. "It may be in many different pieces, but those pieces can still be put back together and become stronger than ever before."

The Chief closed his eyes and looked inward. He told the Buffalo, "I know if I do not sign the treaty, our enemy will come to wipe us out. Many would say it is better to die a warrior's death than surrendering to live a coward's life."

"Yes, many would say that," the Buffalo agreed. "But what do you say, Little Chief?"

"I do not want to watch my people die," the Chief admitted. "I also do not want to watch them die on the inside because we are stuck on a reservation, unable to live free in the way we have always lived."

"There would be many changes for your people living on a reservation. They would have to change, too."

"We do not want to change!" the Chief cried. "I do not want to change! My people have lived a certain way since before my great-great-grandfather was chief. If we are forced to change, we would no longer be Lakota. Maybe it would be better to fight and die. At least we would fight and die as who we are now."

"Everything changes, Little Chief," the Buffalo said calmly. "Look at the children of your tribe – do they not grow older and change? What about the flowers and trees? They change with the seasons, blooming and dying and being reborn. The weather is always changing – sometimes the sun shines, and sometimes the thunderstorms bring rain. The moon changes shape, and the stars change their positions in the sky. Day changes into night, and night into day."

"I understand what you mean, but this is not the same," the Chief insisted. "When the trees go bare in the winter, their leaves return in the spring. The sun disappears when it is the moon's turn to rule the skies, but it always returns at dawn. If my people change, we will change for good. We will become like the White Man and lose everything that makes us Lakota."

"Do you think death would be better than that?" the Buffalo asked.

The Chief shook his head, but there was anger in his voice when he said, "No, death would not be better. But how can I live knowing I am responsible for taking the spirit of my people away?"

"Just because you will change does not mean you will lose everything that makes your people Lakota. You can keep the spirit alive as long as your people still live. You can keep many parts of your culture and pass your memories down to your children. Show them what it means to be Lakota. Share your stories and teach them your rituals. If you do not let that spirit die, no matter what else changes, you will always be Lakota."

"We will always be Lakota," the Chief echoed, thinking deeply about the Great White Buffalo's words.

"I think you know what choice you will make now," the Buffalo said. "I have watched over your people since the beginning. And I will continue watching over them long after you are gone. Rest easy tonight, Little Chief. Everything will be right when the sun rises again."

The Chief opened his eyes and sat up with a jolt. He looked around, realizing he was back in his teepee. The candle on the table had burned out, but the treaty remained exactly where he'd left it. There was sunlight streaming through the opening of his teepee, and he wondered if his encounter with the Great White Buffalo had all been a dream. However, when he went outside to stretch his legs, the tribesman who stood guard the night before rushed over to him.

"Chief! I was about to gather a search party to go find you," the tribesman told him. "I never saw you return last night."

"Everything is fine. There is no need to worry," the Chief assured him. "I have made my decision about the treaty. I will sign it, and we will leave these lands for the last time. But no matter what changes, we will keep the spirit of our tribe alive in our hearts and minds. We will forever be Lakota."

Kohana's First Buffalo Hunt

Kohana gripped his bow tightly and made sure his arrows were within reach in his quiver. His horse neighed and shook its head, mirroring his own anxiousness. This was going to be his first buffalo hunt. After today, he would be seen as a man. However, while he had no trouble hitting the targets when practicing with his bow, a charging buffalo would not be as easy. The hunters hadn't even started riding, yet his heart was already beating as fast as the drums during the previous night's ceremony.

"Try to remain calm," said Akecheta.

He was their tribe's best hunter. Akecheta killed his first buffalo when he was only ten years old, and he'd been leading the buffalo hunts for the last five years. Kohana nodded and tried to do as the older man suggested, but it wasn't simple. The last of the hunters finally mounted their horses, and the party was ready to head off across the plains.

"Ride hard, aim true, and make the kills clean," Akecheta commanded. "Now we go!"

A dozen sets of hooves stomped against the ground and sounded like thunder. Kohana kicked at his horse and sent it galloping along with the rest of the group. He was a skilled rider, so he was able to keep up with the more seasoned hunters. They followed the tracks left by the buffalo and soon caught up with the herd. Seeing them up close as they stampeded with their powerful legs was very different from seeing one brought back following the hunt. Kohana's nerves were on edge, and he feared his hands would shake too much to make a good shot.

Akecheta brought his horse beside Kohana's and shouted, "Look for a straggler! Aim for the neck! You can do this!"

With the older man's encouragement, Kohana scanned the herd to find a buffalo lagging behind the others. The moment he spotted a smaller one struggling to stay with the pack, he turned his horse and took off. This was his chance to prove himself to the tribe. He reached for an arrow from his quiver and set it against his bowstring. Pulling the arrow back, he aimed carefully and released it. The arrow soared through the air and plunged into the side of the smaller buffalo's neck. It groaned loudly as it toppled to the ground, sliding a foot or two through the tall grass before stopping.

"Good shot, Kohana!" Akecheta exclaimed. "You got it!"

Kohana slowed his horse and rode around the slain buffalo to make sure it was dead. He got off his horse and kneeled beside the creature, placing his hand on top of its head. Closing his eyes, he offered a short blessing, saying, "May your spirit find peace with the ancestors and your body be a great boon to my people. I thank you for your sacrifice, so that my people may eat your meat, use your bones in our crafts, and use your hide to stay warm."

At the end of the hunt, the party returned to their village with three buffalo, including the one killed by Kohana. He was beaming a smile at his people as they congratulated him. Their chief emerged from his teepee and embraced Kohana.

"You have proven your skills as a hunter, young one," the chief said. "You are now a man."

Iktómi (The Spider)

Iktómi is a trickster spirit in Lakota culture who usually appears in the form of a spider. However, he has the ability to shapeshift into any form he wants. Sometimes, he shapeshifts into the form of a human and can be recognized by the red, white, and yellow paint he wears and the black rings he has around his eyes. Many of the stories involving Iktómi include morals and lessons to help guide the children of the tribe in behaving the right way. He is also credited as the creator of the first dreamcatcher, spinning his webs to make a net that prevents bad spirits from reaching the sleeping humans.

The Spider and the Oak Tree

Iktómi was sleeping on a web he'd spun between the branches of an old oak tree. He was dreaming a pleasant dream when his web suddenly shook violently. Waking up in a daze, he looked around to see what was causing everything to shake. When he glanced down toward the ground, he saw a young Lakota man hacking at the tree trunk with an axe.

"What do you think you are doing?" Iktómi cried. "You are destroying my home!"

The Lakota man looked up at him and replied, "Quiet! You are a spider and can spin your web anywhere. My people need the wood from this tree to feed our fires and carve our totem poles."

This made Iktómi angry, and he shouted back, "You are a man and can cut down any tree you want! Go cut down another tree and leave my home alone!"

"There are no trees bigger than this one anywhere around here," the man argued. "This was the one my chief told me to cut down. I must obey my chief, so you must find somewhere else to put your web."

Iktómi transformed into a field sparrow and flew away, cursing the Lakota man for stealing his home. He wanted revenge, and he knew exactly how to get it. Soaring over the plains, he searched the lands below for the instrument of his vengeance. As soon as he spotted it, he dived toward the ground. Just before he slammed into the earth, he stretched out his wings to halt his descent. At the last moment, he transformed into a black wolf and landed softly on his paws. The gray-furred leader of the buffalo wolf pack Iktómi was seeking came forward to confront him.

"Who are you, and what are you doing here?" the Wolf Chief asked, showing his fangs in a threatening manner.

"You know who I am," Iktómi said in the Wolf's language. "I helped your father escape a trap that the White Man hid near the river."

"You are Iktómi?" the Wolf questioned, suspicious of the newcomer. "Prove it."

"As you wish." The black wolf transformed into a spider right before the other's eyes. Iktómi then turned back into a wolf. "Satisfied?"

"Very well. I believe you now, Iktómi," said the Wolf Chief. "Why have you come to my pack?"

Iktómi grinned, showing rows of razor-sharp teeth. "The Lakota who live just over those hills have been planning a hunt. They want wolf fur to decorate their teepees and keep them warm when the winter comes. I heard them say they will come for you at dawn tomorrow. But if you strike first..."

"They will never see it coming." the Wolf said, finishing the spider's sentence. "Thank you, Iktómi, for giving us this warning. We will not waste it."

Iktómi transformed into a swallow again and flew away, congratulating himself on his clever plan. The wolves would attack the Lakota village in the night, and those responsible for cutting down his tree would surely be killed. He traveled across the plains until he reached the village, perching atop the largest teepee. It belonged to the Lakota chief, the man who ordered Iktómi's home to be felled.

When the sun disappeared and the moon rose into the sky, Iktómi prepared for the wolf pack's arrival. Clouds covered the night sky, blocking out the stars and the moon. The only light came from the fire burning at the center of the village. Iktómi spat at the Lakota, knowing the wood keeping the flames alive came from his own tree. After most of the tribe were fast asleep, the wolves finally stalked to the edge of the village. They looked angry and merciless.

The wolves charged forward, overwhelming the guards and keeping an eye out for danger. They stormed through the village, tearing down teepees and ripping the Lakota apart. The Wolf Chief thundered into the Lakota chief's teepee and tore out his throat, much to Iktómi's delight. He even got involved, changing into his wolf form and getting his revenge on the man who had chopped down his tree. When the pack had finished their grisly work, they met back up at the center of the village.

"Chief, I saw no weapons or hunting gear in this place," a young wolf said. "Their horses do not look like they are prepared to ride at dawn."

"I saw none of that, either," a she-wolf added. "The only blades were those used to carve totem poles."

"You mean to say you believe the Lakota were not going to attack us?" the Wolf Chief asked. Nearly all of his pack agreed that there were no signs that the tribe presented any danger to them. The Wolf Chief turned to the black wolf and growled, "Did you trick us, Iktómi? Was everything you told me a lie?"

"They destroyed my home and deserved this fate," Iktómi stated proudly. "You should not feel bad about killing them."

The Wolf Chief snarled at him angrily. "What do you mean they destroyed your home? Do you not live wherever you spin your webs?"

"I spun my web in an old oak tree," Iktómi replied. "They cut it down."

"We have lived in peace with the Lakota for years," the Wolf told him. "As long as we kept our distance, they left us alone. Now, you have made us slaughter our neighbors for the offense of chopping down a tree? You do not stay in one place for more than a few days. As you would be going somewhere else soon anyway, why did you not simply leave?"

"Why should I have to leave the tree? They could have chosen another one to cut down."

"Perhaps they should have," the Wolf said. "But tricking us into killing them was not a reasonable response. You have not just caused harm to them – you have harmed my pack as well. Now we will live with the shame of knowing we killed these people for no good reason."

"It is too late to take it back," Iktómi pointed out. "Why feel guilty for something that is already done?"

"Because what we did was not justified. What you tricked us into doing was murder." The Wolf Chief lowered his head and looked like he was ready to spring at any moment. "You will pay for this evil you brought upon us!"

Iktómi laughed and transformed into a swallow, flapping his wings as he flew toward the sky. To his surprise, the Wolf Chief leaped into the air and snatched Iktómi by his legs. The Wolf's fangs bit clean through them, and while Iktómi escaped, he was deeply wounded. When he found a new tree in which to spin his web, he was a spider with only six legs. Iktómi remembered the Wolf Chief's words every time he felt the pain from his wounds. He realized the Wolf was right. While his actions were evil, the Wolf could have killed him, but instead, he only took a part of him. The punishment did not go further than the crime.

Young Man Afraid of His Horses (Tashun-Kakokipa)[6]

Chapter Round-Up Activity

Sometimes, you'll hear information that doesn't sound quite right. Can you figure out the difference between real and fake facts? Think about everything you've read in this chapter and see if you can tell whether the following statements are true or false:

1. The Lakota live in longhouses.
2. The Hunkpapa fought on the side of the United States during the American Indian Wars.
3. Seven subtribes make up the Lakota.
4. The Sans Arc people marked their arrows so nobody else could claim the buffalo they killed.
5. Lakota boys could join in on the buffalo hunts as young as ten years old.
6. Sitting Bull was a member of the Hunkpapa subtribe of the Lakota.
7. Iktómi is the name of a powerful wolf spirit in Lakota mythology.
8. Some members of the Sioux Nation originally lived in the Great Plains before being forced to move to reservations.
9. The Lakota targeted the buffalo at the head of a stampeding herd.
10. Crazy Horse fought against the United States Army during the Battle of Gettysburg.

Answers

1. False
2. True
3. True
4. False
5. True
6. True
7. False
8. True
9. False
10. False

Chapter 3: Pueblo Spirits: Kachinas and the Art of Storytelling

The Pueblo people are Native Americans who live in the Southwestern part of the United States, mostly in New Mexico, Arizona, Texas, and Colorado. Tribes that are considered Puebloans include the Hopi, Acoma, Taos, Isleta, and Zuni. They are known as the Pueblo people because they traditionally live in adobe structures called pueblos. Living in the dry, arid heat of the southwestern deserts means that getting enough rain to support the growing of crops is very important, and the Pueblo tribes have many customs and rituals to encourage rainfall. Rain dances and kachinas dedicated to bringing the rain are popular across every Puebloan tribe.

Kachinas

In the religious beliefs of the Pueblo people, a "kachina" is the name used for cultural spirit beings who serve as protectors and help bring good fortune to the community. The kachinas have three parts: a supernatural spirit, a kachina dancer, and a kachina doll. The kachina dancers perform dance rituals during Pueblo ceremonies, wearing masks and body paint to help channel the kachina spirits. Kachina dolls are carved wooden figures painted with bright colors given to Pueblo children. The kachina dolls help them learn about the different kachina spirits, allowing Pueblo children to recognize the spirits on sight.

The kachina spirits are believed to be the ancestors of the Pueblo people, and they are said to live in the underworld for half the year while spending the other half on Earth with their descendants. Puebloans depend on kachinas to aid the community by bringing rainfall, encouraging crop growth, keeping family members safe, and blessing sources of food. Kachinas can be represented by symbols of animals, cultural objects, or important members of the tribe, like a chief or priestess. Many Puebloans keep kachina dolls in their homes to ask for protection from a specific kachina spirit and teach their family about the kachinas important to them.

The Little Lost Kachina Doll

One day, a child of the Hopi tribe was sent by his parents to fetch water from the river. He followed the path from his village to the river's edge, but a terrible thunderstorm rolled in while he was filling his buckets. The rain poured down and made it hard to see, while the wind whipped around him, making it hard to move. Knowing there was no way he would be able to get back home through the storm, he was forced to find shelter in a nearby cave. After sitting his water buckets down near the entrance, he explored the cave while waiting out the storm.

Near the back of the cave, the child noticed a tiny, strange-looking figure lying on the ground. He picked it up and inspected it, turning it over in his hand. It was made of wood from a Douglas fir, had a painted blue face, a red leather tunic trimmed with white fur, and two large black bird wings. The child recognized it as a kachina doll, almost identical to the one his family had hanging up in their pueblo. His parents had taught him that this kachina was known as the Crow Mother, who was a protector of young children.

A crack of thunder boomed outside, and a flash of lightning lit up the cave. To the child's horror, he saw a red-eyed coyote snarling at him. It bared its razor-sharp fangs at him and let out a howl. The child was frozen in fear, unable to move or run for his life. All he could do was clutch the kachina doll to his chest. Suddenly, a gust of wind filled the cave, swirling around, lifting the dirt and creating a small tornado. As quickly as it appeared, the wind came to a halt, and from the cloud of dirt it left behind, a large figure emerged.

The child looked on in awe as the figure stepped forward to challenge the coyote. She looked exactly like the Crow Mother kachina doll but was almost twice as tall as him. Her wings flapped and forced the coyote back. It howled at the Crow Mother and dug its claws into the ground. Despite its best efforts, it couldn't fight back and turned to flee from the cave, disappearing into the storm. The Crow Mother turned to face the child and laid her hand on his shoulder, removing the chill from his soul and filling him with warmth. There was another blast of thunder and a flash of lightning so bright the child was forced to cover his eyes.

When the child could see again, the Crow Mother was gone. Even the kachina doll he'd been holding had disappeared. Luckily, the rain stopped falling, and the child was able to leave the cave with the buckets of water he'd filled at the river. He hurried back home to his village, checking over his shoulder to make sure the coyote hadn't followed him. After reaching his family's pueblo, he gave the water buckets to his parents and went straight to the Crow Mother kachina doll hanging on the wall. He bowed his head to the figure and whispered, "Thank you for protecting me."

The Zuni Rain Dance Ceremony

The sun streamed in through Lucita's bedroom window and woke her up. After wiping the sleep from her eyes, she looked at the calendar and saw that it was the 19th of August, the day of her tribe's annual rain dance ceremony! She leaped out of bed, more excited than usual. This was the first year she would be allowed to participate in the ceremony. Leading up to the rain dance, she double-checked that everything was in order, not wanting anything to go wrong.

When the time came for the ceremony to begin, Lucita emerged from her home dressed in the traditional clothing all women wear to perform the rain dance; a long black dress with a white embroidered underskirt that showed a few inches at the bottom, a bright Spanish shawl with alternating red and yellow colors in an arrowhead pattern, two square over-shawls, one colored black and the other white, both having a red and white striped border and an ornately-decorated kachina mask that was shaped like an eagle. No part of her body or face was showing beneath her outfit besides her bare feet.

Lucita joined the tribe members and participated in the ceremony at the center of her village. She got into the line behind the other women, standing about four feet away from the line of men. The high priest of the tribe came out and offered a blessing to the kachina spirits before kicking off the ceremony. Lucita and the other kachina dancers began their rain dance routine. She followed their rhythm, stepping with her left foot, then a little further with her right. Slowly, the rain dancers inched their way forward, moving in groups of three around two sides of the four-sided quadrangle of the village center.

Although the male rain dancers had fiercer energy in their steps, the female dancers moved more gracefully. Lucita felt like she was ebbing and flowing along the current of a river, swirling around in her kachina costume. The energy of the spirits filled her body, and it was as if they were controlling her motions. Every step she took and dance move she executed wasn't just her calling out to the heavens for the rain to fall. Lucita could see her ancestors and the tribe elders, who had long since passed. They all joined in with the dancers, amplifying the call of the spirits within.

The dancers sang the traditional songs of their tribe, honoring those who came before and those who would arrive in the future. Every dancer got a chance to add their own verse, improvising the lyrics to make a personal appeal to the kachina spirits. When it was Lucita's turn, she knew exactly what she wanted to say. In a powerful voice that came from deep in her soul, she cried out, "We see the corn and the wheat and the grain, we give thanks to the spirits for giving us these gifts! The rivers, sun, and clouds that carry the rain, we give thanks to the wellspring of life on this Earth!"

The rain dance ceremony ended, and it was time for the celebration to begin. The tribe had prepared a great feast to honor the harvest and welcome the autumn months. Many in the village approached Lucita to compliment her on her performance. She wore a smile that stretched from ear to ear, proud of the fact that her first rain dance was a success. When all the food had been eaten, and the cups were bone dry, the stars and the moon came out to play. By the time Lucita returned to her bed, she was ready for a good night's sleep.

As she drifted off, she heard a soft pitter-patter on her roof. It grew louder, battering the roof of her home. Looking out the window, she saw the torrent of rain showering down on the world. The tribe's rain dance had worked; the crops would be well-fed that night! Lucita was very satisfied with that outcome. She had given her heart and soul to the dance, and the spirits accepted this offering as payment for bringing the rain. Now that the ceremony was over, she looked forward to doing it again when another year had passed.

Chapter Round-Up Activity

How well do you remember the tales told in this chapter? Can you finish these stories in your own words? Take a look at the following sections of the tales you've just read and try to fill in the missing parts (If you're using an e-reader or reading in an e-book format, you can write your responses in a notebook):

1. When the time came for the ceremony to begin, Lucita emerged from her home dressed in the traditional clothing all women wear to perform the rain dance:

   _____

   _____

   _____

   _____

2. Near the back of the cave, the child noticed a tiny, strange-looking figure lying on the ground. He picked it up and inspected it, turning it over in his hand. It was made of wood from a Douglas fir, had a painted blue face, a red leather tunic trimmed with white fur, and two large black bird wings. The child recognized it as

   _____

   _____

   _____

   _____

3. The kachina spirits are believed to be the ancestors of the Pueblo people, and they are said to live in

   _____

   _____

   _____

   _____

4. The dancers sang the traditional songs of their tribe, honoring those who came before and those who would arrive in the future. Every dancer got a chance to add their own verse, improvising the lyrics to make a personal appeal to the kachina spirits. When it was Lucita's turn, she knew exactly what she wanted to say. In a powerful voice that came from deep in her soul, she cried out,

_____

_____

_____

_____

_____

5. When the child could see again, the Crow Mother was gone. Even the kachina doll he'd been holding had disappeared. Luckily, the rain stopped falling, and the child could leave the cave with the buckets of water he'd filled at the river. He hurried back home to his village, checking over his shoulder to make sure the coyote didn't follow him. After reaching his family's pueblo, he gave the water buckets to his parents and went straight to the Crow Mother kachina doll hanging on the wall. He

_____

_____

_____

_____

_____

Chapter 4: Cherokees: The Trail of Tears and Resistance

The Cherokee Nation is a tribe of Native Americans who lived in the Southeastern Woodlands of the United States, mostly in Virginia, North Carolina, South Carolina, Georgia, Tennessee, and Alabama. After the Indian Removal Act of 1830, the Cherokee were forced to endure a long and deadly trek from their homelands to the Indian Territory west of the Mississippi River. This event was known as the Trail of Tears, and it involved the forced relocation of five major tribes, which the United States called the "Five Civilized Tribes," including the Cherokee, Chickasaw, Muscogee, Choctaw, and Seminole tribes.

The Seal of the Cherokee Nation.[6]

The Trail of Tears

The Trail of Tears lasted from 1830 (when the Indian Removal Act was signed into law by United States President Andrew Jackson) until 1850. During those twenty years, over 60,000 Native Americans from the Five Civilized Tribes were forcibly moved from their native lands to the Indian Territory, which was designated specifically for the Native Americans. No matter which part of the country the Native Americans originally lived in, they were sent west of the Mississippi River to a portion of what are now the states of Arkansas and Oklahoma. The journey from their homelands to the Indian Territory was dangerous for those forced to make it, stretching across more than 5,000 miles, and between 13,200 and 16,700 people died from disease and warfare along the way.

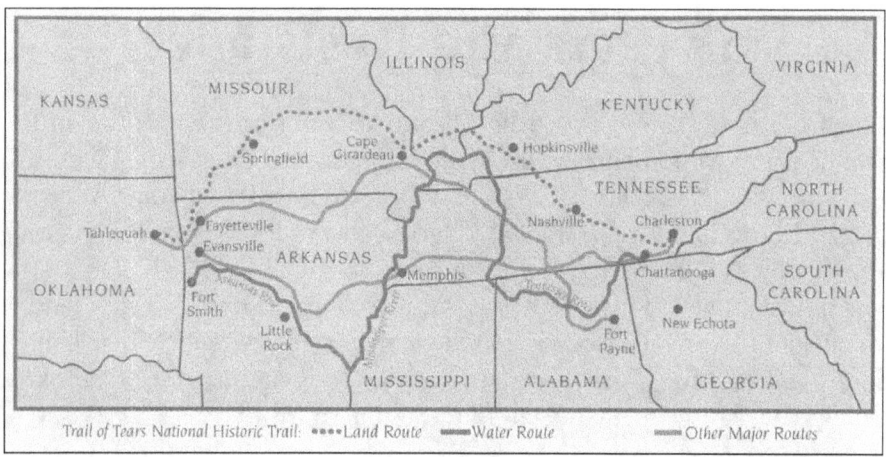

The Trail of Tears.'

Not all Native Americans simply accepted their forced removal and relocation. Some groups fought back against the United States government, with many resistance movements erupting into violence. The Seminole tribe refused to submit to the Indian Removal Act, having already been fighting against being forced onto reservations. The Seminole Wars first broke out in 1816, and they continued all the way until 1858. Smaller collections of other tribes also resisted, including about 100 Cherokees. Despite their best efforts, they were unable to stop the Trail of Tears from happening, and, in the end, all their land was taken by the United States.

Cherokee Culture

The Cherokee Nation was traditionally made up of "red towns" and "white towns." The red towns were meant for warriors and had a supreme war chief as their top leader. The white towns were for the peaceful tribe members, and they were led by a supreme peace chief. The Cherokee living in red towns were known for their elaborate war ceremonies, while the white towns gave wrongdoers a safe place to live. Together, the two types of towns provided the Cherokees with the ability to fight and defend their people and places where those who wanted to avoid conflict could go.

A major part of Cherokee culture was the weaving of baskets and making of pottery. They grew corn (called "maize"), squash, and beans to feed their people. Their hunters brought back hides, furs, and antlers from bears, deer, and elk to create furniture and decorate their homes. Those homes were mostly log cabins with tree bark roofs, and they had a single door, a smoke hole in the roof, and no windows in the walls. The average Cherokee town had between 30 to 60 homes and a larger council house where the tribe could hold meetings and burn the sacred fire during ceremonies.

Tears of a Child

For the first nine years of her life, Inola had lived with her family in the vibrant green lands of Georgia. Now, she was being forced to leave it all behind: her friends, her home, and all the spirits she'd come to know while wandering through the grasslands and forests. She said goodbye to the jagged rocks, the towering trees, the babbling brook, and the soft dirt that she'd come to know so well. Inola could feel the sadness around her as she bid them all farewell. Even the skies wept for her. The raindrops splattered against the ground as her family began their journey to the new lands where they would live.

"Mother, I do not want to go," Inola said sadly.

"We have to go, child," her mother replied. "The White Men have threatened to burn down our homes and shoot us with their guns if we do not follow their orders."

Everything Inola's family owned was being carried on their backs. They had to leave behind their furniture and decorations, including her favorite painted pot. It was too big to fit in their packs and would have taken up too much room. Her father and older brother carried most of their belongings, but her mother was hauling her fair share of the burden. Even Inola had a pack strapped to her back, filled with a handful of her own things. She hugged her corn husk doll to her chest and tried to ignore the aching in her legs. Her mother warned her they would need to walk ten miles daily to reach the Indian Territory within four months. She couldn't imagine having to walk that far, but she tried to look at it as a grand adventure.

Many other Cherokee families were traveling from one side of the Mississippi River to the other. Some had wagons, but most were forced to go on foot, like Inola's family. Her father and brother hunted for animals, while Inola and her mother picked berries and nuts. As they traveled along the trail, they discovered it became harder to find food since so many other Cherokees were walking the same path and taking food from the same places. Luckily, her father was one of the tribe's best hunters, and he always managed to track and kill something for them to eat.

The rain made the ground muddy, and Inola had trouble walking through it. Her mother held her hand and helped her along the way, but it slowed the family down. They watched the other Cherokees pass by them, and Inola felt guilty that she was making the journey take longer than it should be. Her father set up a basic camp for them at night, but it was only a small fire and blankets made from the bear he killed while out hunting three years ago. There were only two blankets, so Inola's father and brother had only the campfire to keep them warm.

A week into the trip, the family reached Fort Payne in Alabama. The White Men from the United States Army herded the Cherokees like cattle through the fort, sending them on their way. Inola and her family spent the night camped outside the fort, packed with hundreds of her people, seeking to find some extra food that the soldiers had stored away. A few dozen soldiers stepped over the Cherokees as they gave out some bread and corn. One soldier took pity on Inola's brother and gave him a small blanket made of woven wool. The next day, they followed the other members of their tribe as the soldiers pushed them to continue on their journey.

Inola's family headed north, crossing the border into Tennessee. The land became harder to walk on, as hills began to rise and fall as they left Alabama. It seemed to her that the weather was harsher, and it was getting colder at night. She felt tired all the time now, as her entire life was nothing but walking, eating, and sleeping. However, her sleep was far from restful, and she no longer woke up feeling refreshed. As they got closer to Memphis, Inola's brother developed a nasty cough. He got weaker and weaker, to the point that his mother began carrying part of his load. It wasn't long before he could barely keep himself upright, and the family was forced to leave behind part of their precious few belongings.

Seven miles outside of Memphis, Inola's family got caught in a snowstorm that rolled through the area. They took shelter in a small cave to wait out the storm. In the morning, after the snow had stopped falling, Inola's father dug them out with his hands. When he cleared a path to let them escape, two of his fingers were completely blue and swollen. He couldn't feel them anymore, and his wife realized he'd got frostbite. Not wanting to delay their travels more than they had to, Inola's father woke her brother up so they could go.

"Wake up, boy – we must leave this cave," her father said. He nudged his son with his good hand, but Inola's brother would not get up. Her brother didn't move, either. In fact, he wasn't moving at all. To her horror, her father announced to the family, "Our boy is dead."

He dug a grave for Inola's brother inside the cave since the soil outside was frozen and too hard to break. Since her brother didn't bring anything that was just his own, they buried him with the blanket given to him by the soldier at the fort. Her mother wanted it gone anyway because she blamed it for getting him sick. There was no feast, no celebration of his life, and they remained at his graveside only long enough to offer a short prayer. Inola's father assured his mother that the spirits would understand. If they didn't leave soon, they would all die in that cave.

Trudging through the snow was a miserable experience for Inola. She and her mother kept their blankets wrapped around themselves, but her father had only his regular clothing to protect him. He led the way, pushing aside as much of the snow as he could to make it easier for the rest of his family to walk. Inola carefully stepped into her father's footprints to avoid sinking her feet into the snow. As the hours passed, she noticed his footprints were getting closer together, and she could tell he was exhausted. However, he refused to stop until they reached the city.

The family finally made it to Memphis. Inola was in awe, looking up at the large buildings and factories chugging thick black smoke from the metal smokestacks. She tried to imagine what kind of fires could create smoke like that. She knew the only large buildings with large fires were the lodges where great council meetings took place, so she assumed they must serve the same purpose for the White Men. Although she had hoped her family would get to spend the night inside one of the many buildings that littered the city, they didn't have any money, and the White Men refused to barter. They were forced to sleep in an encampment with their fellow Cherokees and other tribes.

Inola and her family spent several days in the city waiting for the snow to melt. She watched the White Men in their strange, heavy clothing rush around all day. People streamed into the factories and came back out at night looking red-faced and dirty. Many of them went directly to the taverns, which were filled with a mixture of laughter and shouts. Some of the White Men ended up getting into scuffles outside the taverns, and Inola witnessed one man get shot with a gun. She couldn't understand how they lived in a place like that. It was crowded, loud, and suffocating. No matter how hard she tried, she couldn't feel the presence of the spirits anywhere.

After noticing another group of people she'd never seen before, Inola asked her mother, "Who are those people with skin darker than ours?"

"They are slaves. They are owned by the White Men," her mother explained.

"How can the White Men own them?" Inola asked in confusion. "We are all born free, so we can live in balance with nature."

"The White Men take many things that do not belong to them," her mother said. "That includes the freedom of the dark-skinned people from across the sea."

When it came time to leave the city, Inola's father had managed to get some food to take with them. His fingers hadn't healed from the frostbite, and he feared that he wouldn't be able to draw arrows in his bow as well as he did before. That would make it harder for him to hunt, and fewer things grew in the harsher winters of these lands. The family returned to the trail and soon crossed the Mississippi River into Arkansas. They had to wait almost an entire day to use the White Men's ferries to take them across the raging waters, as it was too deep and dangerous to ford on foot.

Their trip through Arkansas stretched on for weeks. When they ran out of food, Inola's father went hunting despite his injured fingers. Upon his return, he apologized for only managing to kill a small rabbit. Still, they were grateful to have anything to eat. Inola's father took only a single bite of meat before handing it to her, and then he went to sleep. In the morning, he looked tired and weaker than she'd ever seen him, but he insisted that he was fine. However, when they loaded their packs, he couldn't lift his own, and they were again forced to leave some of their belongings behind.

Inola's family reached another place settled by the White Men called Evansville, but it wasn't anything like Memphis. This was a small trading post town, and to her father's surprise, the owner of the trading post was actually willing to barter. Instead of giving the trading post owner money in exchange for food, her father traded a few of their remaining belongings for it. Inola's mother had to give up her bear skin blanket, as it was the only item the trader really seemed to want. That at least got them plenty of food to last the rest of their journey, as long as there were no more delays.

Only a few days after leaving the trading post, Inola's father became nervous, constantly looking over his shoulder and scanning their surroundings like he did while hunting. Her parents kept whispering to each other, but she couldn't hear what they were saying. When the family was camped out for the night, her father refused to sleep and held his bow across his lap. At some point, she was awakened by shouting and opened her eyes to find three Chickasaw men rushing toward their camp. Her father was firing arrows at them, but he could not hit his marks. They soon reached him, and although he fought as well as he could, they overpowered him in the end. One Chickasaw plunged a knife into his neck, and they grabbed the family's stockpile of food before disappearing into the night.

There was nothing Inola's mother could do to save her husband, and by morning, he was dead. She and her daughter dug a grave for him and buried him with his bow. As with Inola's brother, they didn't feast and had nothing to celebrate. As soon as they offered prayers to the spirits, they packed up what little they had left and could carry. Inola's mother had tucked a small bit of food away in her own pack, which the Chickasaw thieves managed to overlook. They set out again, their family now half the size it was when they left their home.

Inola and her mother moved slower than before and stopped more often. Her mother insisted on giving their remaining food to her daughter while keeping only a few bites for herself. Inola watched her mother wasting away before her eyes, but her mother's spirit was fierce. They had made it to the Indian Territory. They were only a couple of days away from Tahlequah, the new capital of the Cherokee Nation. The moment Inola spotted the large village in the distance, she shouted for joy.

Her mother smiled weakly and said, "Go, child. You can make it from here on your own. Do not wait for me."

"Why must I go alone?" Inola asked. "We are so close. Our people will give us food and shelter."

Her mother never answered. She collapsed to the ground, and no matter what Inola did, she couldn't wake her back up. Refusing to leave her mother, she sat there on the ground for hours, pleading with her mother to wake up. A pair of Cherokee hunters stumbled upon them. They knew immediately that Inola's mother was dead. The hunters were kind to Inola and helped her bury her mother's body, then took her to Tahlequah with them. They took her to the village's chief, and he listened to her tell him about all that her family had suffered and endured throughout their journey. When Inola had finished speaking, she burst out crying. She couldn't hold in the sorrow any longer.

"We will take care of you, child, for you are one of us," the chief assured her. "This new land is different, but we are still Cherokee. We do not abandon our own."

"Thank you, chief," Inola said between sobs.

The chief's wife took Inola by the hand and led her away to find something to eat and somewhere to sleep. The chief sighed sadly as he watched Inola go. She was far from the first to tell him such a tale, and he feared many more would come.

He turned to his shaman advisor and stated, "Those of our people do not need to follow a trail of footprints to find this new land. They only need to follow the trail of tears we have left behind."

Chapter Round-Up Activity

How much were you able to learn from this chapter? Can you pick out the right answer from multiple choices? See if you can find the correct response to the following questions:

1. What year did President Andrew Jackson sign the Indian Removal Act into law?
    a. 1848
    b. 1830
    c. 1819
    d. 1854

2. What is part of the Cherokee people's funeral customs?
    a. They bury their dead in graves
    b. They have a feast and celebration
    c. They leave belongings in the graves
    d. All of the above

3. How many windows were in a typical Cherokee cabin?
    a. 4
    b. 0
    c. 2
    d. 6

4. Which tribe was NOT considered part of the "Five Civilized Tribes?"
    a. Cherokee
    b. Muscogee
    c. Lakota
    d. Seminole

5. About how many Native Americans were forced to endure the Trail of Tears?
    a. 60,000
    b. 45,000
    c. 100,000
    d. 86,000

6. What was the name of the Cherokee capital in the Indian Territory?
    a. Memphis
    b. New Echota
    c. Tahlequah
    d. Fort Payne
7. What type of crop was NOT grown by the Cherokee people?
    a. Potatoes
    b. Maize
    c. Squash
    d. Beans
8. Which two colors were used for the Cherokee's war and peace towns?
    a. Blue and Yellow
    b. Red and White
    c. White and Green
    d. Red and Yellow
9. What future state was the Indian Territory located in?
    a. Nevada
    b. Georgia
    c. Kansas
    d. Oklahoma
10. How many homes were in a typical Cherokee village?
    a. 40 to 50
    b. 25 to 35
    c. 15 to 45
    d. 30 to 60

Answers

1. b.
2. d.
3. b.
4. c.
5. a.
6. c.
7. a.
8. b.
9. d.
10. d.

Chapter 5: Iroquois (Haudenosaunee) Confederacy: The Great Law of Peace

The Iroquois or Haudenosaunee Confederacy was originally made up of five tribes, and after 1722, six tribes. They were also known as the Five or Six Nations by the English colonists. The Confederacy was different from other tribes or alliances at the time because they had a system in place to give each member tribe a voice in the decisions they made. Rather than having a single chief, each tribe voted for which members would get a seat on the Grand Council, and those elected members then represented their tribe in discussions and decisions made by the Council.

Before 1722, the Iroquois Confederacy was made up of the Seneca, Cayuga, Oneida, Onondaga, and Mohawk tribes. In 1722, they added the Tuscarora tribe to the Confederacy. At the height of their power and influence, the Iroquois' lands stretched from Ontario and Quebec in Canada to the Northeastern United States, going as far south as the Allegheny Mountains in Virginia. They also held territory in the states of New York, Pennsylvania, West Virginia, Ohio, and Kentucky. The Iroquois mostly lived along the shores of lakes and the banks of rivers, such as the Great Lakes and the Ohio River.

Flag of the Iroquois Confederacy.*

Longhouses

Longhouses were an important part of Iroquois culture. The name they used for themselves was "Haudenosaunee," which means "people of the longhouse." The Iroquois lived in longhouses made from wooden poles, which were created by cutting down tree saplings and using fire to remove all the moisture from them so they would become harder. They sharpened one end of the poles so they could drive them into the ground like stakes, securing the walls of their homes. The roofs were made from poles bent into arcs with grass and leaves covering the top, and both the walls and roof used poles set from the front to the back of the longhouse to keep them sturdy.

An average longhouse was 80 feet long, 18 feet wide, and 18 feet high. They were meant to shelter many families, sometimes as many as twenty, in a single longhouse. Most of these families were related in some way through the female members, such as sons and daughters of the same mother, grandchildren of the same grandmother, or the families of sisters. There were also larger longhouses built to serve as meeting places to hold celebrations and discuss tribal matters. When it came time for tribes to elect representatives to sit on the Grand Council of the Iroquois Confederacy and speak for their people, the voting often happened in the larger longhouses.

Wampum Belts

A wampum is a type of shell bead shaped like a tube that was used by the Iroquois to create belts and jewelry. These shell beads could be many different colors, and the Iroquois developed a system that allowed them to use specific combinations of colored wampum to represent words and ideas. Wampum belts were woven with colored bead shells with designs that could be read by anyone who knew the wampum language system. The Iroquois used wampum belts to keep records of events and the treaties they made.

The Great Peacemaker

Long ago, before the White Men came to the New World, there were many Native American tribes living throughout the unspoiled lands. However, not all of them got along, and there were five tribes in the northeastern part of the New World that were constantly at war. The Seneca, Cayuga, Oneida, Onondaga, and Mohawk tribes seemed to hate each other. Whenever there was a short time of peace, it soon ended, and they were back to fighting. The people just accepted that this was how things were, believing it was how things would always be.

Far to the north, a tribe known as the Huron lived apart from the other tribes. There was a woman among them whom the others found strange, and none of the men wanted to marry her. The women of the tribe bullied her, and the men made fun of her, causing her to go off on her own. Since she was not married and lived away from the rest of her tribe, she was shocked when she woke up one day to find that she was pregnant. She thanked the spirits for this miracle because it meant she would no longer be alone.

After giving birth, the Huron woman named her baby Dekanawida, which meant "two river currents flowing together." She chose that name because she strongly believed that he was going to grow up to do something important and sit at the point where the destinies of others would meet. Dekanawida wasn't raised like the other children of the Huron tribe. His mother didn't want him to be a warrior. She wanted him to be a force for peace. Whenever he spoke to the other people of his tribe, they looked down on him for trying to get them to abandon their warlike ways.

When Dekanawida got older, he truly understood why his mother preached peace over war. He went south to hunt for food and stumbled upon a battlefield after a fight between the Mohawks and Oneidas. What he found horrified him, as he'd never seen so much death before in his life. There was a Mohawk warrior collecting war trophies, and Dekanawida asked him why the two tribes had fought.

"I do not remember," the Mohawk warrior said. "That is just the way it is."

Later, Dekanawida caught up to an Oneida warrior limping back to his village. Dekanawida asked him the same question.

"I do not remember," answered the Oneida warrior. "That is just the way it is."

Dekanawida couldn't believe that the tribes were willing to kill each other when they didn't even know why they wanted the other side to die. They had simply become so used to war that the idea of *not* killing each other never entered their minds. However, he also knew that his message of peace would not be received very well if he approached the tribes alone. His own tribe dismissed every attempt he made to teach them about peace. There was no way he'd be successful with the rival tribes.

When Dekanawida reached adulthood, his mother urged him to leave home and fulfill his destiny. He was doubtful that he could be successful in his mission to bring peace to the tribes, but his mother believed in him. She insisted that he was meant to do great things with his life and that he would someday become important in helping his people in some way.

That night, his mother went outside to meditate beneath a nearby tree. In the morning, she was gone, and Dekanawida searched far and wide, trying to find her. She was nowhere to be found, so he cut down the tree and made it into a canoe when he returned home. He dragged the canoe down to the river and got in, traveling south to the lands of the five rival tribes. Dekanawida was determined to follow through with his mission and make his mother proud. He came up with the Great Law of Peace, a way for enemies to become allies by using peaceful discussions to settle their conflicts instead of going to war.

Reaching the lands of the rival tribes, Dekanawida did his best to spread his message of peace. They laughed at him as he expected, calling him a coward for not wanting to be a warrior, and sent him away. Each of the five tribes gave him the same cold treatment, and he quickly lost hope in ever completing his mission. While journeying across the lands, he stopped to rest at the home of a woman who was known for taking in warriors from every tribe. The warriors would get food and sleep safely because the woman refused to allow them to fight when they were under her roof.

Dekanawida recognized that the woman shared a similar outlook to him. They spoke for hours, with Dekanawida explaining his vision for all the tribes to live in peace. He was inspired by the way she got the enemy warriors to not kill each other when they were in her home, and he told her that he wanted to build a longhouse where the tribes could meet and talk out their problems around the fire, just like they ate and slept in peace around the fire in her home. The woman really liked that idea and promised to support Dekanawida's mission in any way she could. She also changed her name to Jigonhsasee, which meant "new face," to show her devotion to his vision of peace.

Not long after leaving Jigonhsasee's home, Dekanawida spotted a cabin that sat alone in the mountains. He hiked up to the cabin, wanting to meet the person who lived there. The owner of the home was away when he arrived, but there was something cooking in a pot on the fire in the cabin. Dekanawida climbed onto the roof and looked down the smoke hole to see what it was. He was sickened when he discovered that the cabin's owner was cooking people. This was the home of a truly evil person, but Dekanawida thought that if he could convert the man to his vision for peace, he could convince anyone that peace was better than war.

The cabin's owner returned home and went to check on his food. He looked down into the pot, expecting to see his own face reflected in the boiling water. Instead, he saw the reflection of Dekanawida's face staring down the smoke hole. The face he saw didn't look evil like his face, but it looked beautiful, wise, and strong. The man mistook it for his own face, thinking the spirits had transformed him and removed the evil from his soul. However, the face disappeared, and when he looked in the pot again, he saw only his own ugly reflection. This made him feel ashamed, and he was saddened to realize how terrible he'd become.

Hiawatha by Thomas Eakins.[9]

Dekanawida entered the cabin, and the man was surprised to see the face from the cooking pot again. It made him feel even more ashamed that he would never get to know what it was like to be anything other than evil.

"Are you an avenging spirit who has come to kill me for the evil I have done?" the man asked.

"No. I do not believe in killing anyone, no matter how evil they might be," Dekanawida replied. "Tell me your name so I may speak to you properly."

"My name is Hiawatha. I was once an Onondaga, but when they found out about the evil I had done, they sent me away to live alone in the mountains. They forced me to leave my family behind. I have become such a terrible man; my wife and children would not recognize me if they saw me today."

"Hiawatha, I know you have done many evil things," Dekanawida said. "But you can change your ways if you want to."

"I want to change my ways," Hiawatha insisted. "I am tired of having this evil in my soul. I want to see my family again. Tell me what I must do, and I will do it. I no longer wish to hurt others. I want to be like you."

"Then you must spread my message of peace. Return to your people and give them the Great Law of Peace."

Dekanawida told Hiawatha everything about his plans and ideas for a peaceful future. Hiawatha agreed to Dekanawida's terms and returned to his people to spread the message of peace. Dekanawida set off to find more who were willing to accept his vision, feeling more positive about his chances after having convinced Hiawatha to change his evil ways. The men headed out in separate directions – Hiawatha to the Onondaga village and Dekanawida to the Mohawk village.

When Hiawatha reached his old tribe, they weren't happy to see him. He was told that after he was sent away, an evil chief named Tadodaho had taken over. The Onondaga's new chief could use magic, and his body and mind were twisted by the evil spells he cast. Tadodaho had snakes instead of hair – and snakes coming out of his fingers! Hiawatha tried to spread Dekanawida's message of peace, calling the tribe together and suggesting they form a council to rule the tribe instead of a chief. Tadodaho was furious at Hiawatha for trying to take away his power, and he killed the man's wife and three daughters with his magic. Filled with grief at learning about the fate of his family, Hiawatha left the village, wandering the wilderness while mourning his lost loved ones.

Meanwhile, Dekanawida came to the village of the Mohawks and spoke about the Great Law of Peace. They refused to believe they could survive without fighting against the other tribes. They challenged him to prove that the spirits supported his message. He accepted their challenge and climbed a tall tree growing beside a deep gorge. Looking over the edge, he saw the ground was hundreds of feet down. Falling into the gorge was a sure way to die, but the Mohawks told him that if the spirits were on his side, he would survive. They cut down the tree with Dekanawida still in it and watched it fall into the gorge. It appeared to them that the spirits weren't with him, and they returned to their village to prepare for war.

The next morning, the Mohawks were shocked when Dekanawida returned to the village unharmed. Since he survived the fall into the gorge, they decided the spirits must be on his side and support his vision. They finally accepted his message of peace and converted from their warlike ways to become a tribe that solved their problems without violence. After living with the Mohawks and helping them change their ways, a scout found the wandering Hiawatha and brought him back to the village. He explained to Dekanawida about what happened at the Onondaga village and begged Dekanawida to take away his pain. Dekanawida performed a ritual to help Hiawatha and began to chant.

"I wipe away tears from thy face, using the white fawn skin of pity," he said. "I make it daylight for thee. I beautify the sky. Now shall thou do thy thinking in peace."

All those who watched Dekanawida's ritual were amazed to see it work. Hiawatha's grief and pain were lifted from his soul. The pair decided to visit the other tribes to convince them that peace was the right path. The Mohawk's newly-elected leaders went with them, hoping that by showing their rival tribes they had accepted the message of peace, the tribes would do the same. With the Mohawks' support, Dekanawida got the Oneida and Cayuga to join their mission and give peace a chance to improve their lives.

The Seneca were in the middle of a conflict within their tribe when the messengers of peace came to their village. Word had spread of the other tribes laying down their weapons and giving up their wars. Half of the Senecas wanted to join with the peaceful tribes, while the other half felt it was nothing but a trick. It looked like the Senecas were about to go to war with themselves when the outsiders interrupted them. Dekanawida spoke about the Great Law of Peace, but the half of the tribe who still wanted to fight weren't sure it would work. During their discussions, there was a solar eclipse, and seeing the moon block out the sun's light was taken as a sign from the spirits to accept Dekanawida's vision.

Four of the five tribes had joined each other to live peacefully, but the Onondaga remained their enemy. Dekanawida, Hiawatha, and the leaders from the other four tribes returned to the Onondaga village to confront Tadodaho together. When the group arrived at the Onondaga village, the evil chief tried to turn them away. Still, his people were impressed that Dekanawida had convinced enemies to become allies. Dekanawida told Hiawatha to comb the snakes out of Tadodaho's hair while he performed the same ritual he'd used to help Hiawatha. In the end, they removed the evil from Tadodaho, straightening his twisted body and mind as he gave up his evil ways.

With the Onondaga now joined with their alliance, Dekanawida prepared to give a speech in which he would suggest the five tribes combine into a single tribe. They all shared the same ancestors and spoke similar languages, so they had much more in common than they originally believed. However, Dekanawida could not speak publicly because he had a stutter that got worse when he gave speeches to large groups. Hiawatha was skilled at public speaking, so he addressed the tribes in Dekanawida's place. When Hiawatha's speech was over, the five tribes agreed to make their alliance official and created the Iroquois Confederacy.

Now that the Iroquois were a single tribe, they needed to organize it and how their leadership would work. Dekanawida brought in Jigonhsasee – whom he gave the job of assigning roles to their people. She remembered what he'd told her when he stayed at her home, explaining his vision for a peaceful tribe.

"It will take the form of the longhouse in which there are many hearths," he'd stated. "One for each family, yet all live as one household under one chief mother. They shall have one mind and live under one law. Thinking will replace killing, and there shall be one commonwealth."

Jigonhsasee gave the men their positions during the gathering to discuss the Great Law of Peace. They were organized into a Great Council, and each of the five tribes was given seats on the Council. The individual tribes would be allowed to elect the leaders that they wanted to send to sit on the Council. The number of seats given to each tribe was based on their size. The Onondaga got 14 seats, the Cayuga got 10, the Oneida got 9, the Mohawk got 9, and the Seneca got 8. She also assigned the women the right to choose the chief of their longhouses, making them a very important part of the Iroquois tribe.

The Iroquois proclaimed Dekanawida the Great Peacemaker for bringing them together. Jigonhsasee was called the Mother of Nations for her role in organizing the Iroquois Confederacy. Hiawatha was honored for turning away from evil to embrace the message of peace and his ability to deliver that message in great speeches. Without these three people, the five tribes would have never stopped fighting. Without the proof that a confederacy with elected leaders working together to solve their problems was a system that could work, the United States of America might not have existed.

Chapter Round-Up Activity

Want to be like the Iroquois and make your own wampum belt? It's pretty easy to create one yourself. All you need are some basic supplies from a craft store. You can come up with your own designs that represent whatever you want. For example, the design of the Hiawatha Belt represents the five tribes of the original Iroquois Confederacy. The middle shape that looks like an arrowhead represents the Onondaga. The two larger squares represent the Cayuga on the left and the Oneida on the right. The smaller square on the left represents the Seneca and the smaller square on the right represents the Mohawk.

Hiawatha's belt.[10]

To make your own wampum belt, you'll need:

- Colored beads
- Scissors
- Tape
- String

Directions:

1. Cut 3 to 5 lengths of string measuring about one foot each.
2. Place the strings on the table horizontally and an equal distance apart.
3. Slide the colored beads onto the strings, making patterns by matching the same colored beads from one string to another.
4. When you've finished with your beads, push the strings together and wrap the tape around the middle and the ends.
5. Show off your wampum belt and tell everyone what the designs represent.

Chapter 6: Inuit Traditions: Stories on Adapting to Arctic Life

The Inuit people are Native Americans living in North America's Arctic and subarctic parts, such as Alaska, Yukon, Northwest Territories, Quebec, Nunavut, Labrador, and Greenland. They have adapted to survive in the extreme cold, using the natural resources around them to build shelter, make clothing, and find food. Since crops can't grow in the freezing climate where they live, the Inuit people are hunters and fishermen. They have also trained dogs to pull sleds to quickly move across the snowy environments. The Inuit people have a rich tradition of stories and legends passed down from generation to generation.

Inuit people.[11]

The Legend of Sedna

Sedna.[19]

Long ago, a fisherman and his wife had a daughter they named Sedna. They lived in a small Inuit village near the freezing sea. Sedna grew up into a beautiful maiden, and Inuit men came from far-off villages to seek her hand in marriage. Many of her suitors were great hunters or fishermen, and they came with gifts they hoped to give Sedna's father in exchange for his blessing to marry her. The hunters brought furs and hides from their most impressive kills, while the fishermen offered the largest fish they could catch. However, Sedna turned every single one of them down, refusing all their marriage proposals.

Her father became upset that she wouldn't take a husband. He argued that she needed to get married and start a family of her own. The more her father pushed her, the more Sedna pushed back, telling him she might never get married. He exploded with anger and demanded that she choose a husband by the next sunrise, or he would kick her out of his home and leave her outside to freeze to death. She had less than a day to find a husband, yet it should have been easy. Every unmarried man in the village was willing to take Sedna as their wife. All she needed to do was go for a walk and pick the first man she saw.

When the sun rose the following morning, Sedna's father went to see whether she'd found herself a husband. Sedna had a big smile on her face and told him that she was married, and he was thrilled to hear this news. His joy immediately turned into rage when Sedna introduced him to her new husband – she had married the lead dog of the family's dog sled team. Fed up with his daughter's disrespect, he grabbed her by the hair and dragged her out of the house. He pulled her down to the shore, threw her into his kayak, and then took the kayak far out to sea.

Once the kayak was far enough that he was sure Sedna wouldn't be able to swim back, he pushed her overboard. She clung to the side of the kayak, begging him to pull her back up, but he grabbed his knife and sliced off her fingers. She fell into the icy waters and sank to the bottom of the sea. Satisfied that he was rid of his troublesome daughter, the fisherman returned home alone.

Instead of drowning as her father intended, Sedna reached the bottom of the sea and was swallowed up by the earth. She tumbled down into the underworld, which the fearsome monsters called home. They were struck by Sedna's beauty and made her their queen, transforming her into a goddess of the sea. When they turned her into a goddess, her fingers that still floated in the sea became seals, walruses, and whales. From that day on, if she became angry, the sea creatures hunted by the Inuits would disappear, so the tribe's shaman had to go out in kayaks and comb her hair to calm her back down. Only then would the sea creatures return.

Anik the Brave

Anik the Brave.[13]

Anik stood near the wall of his family's igloo and watched nervously as his mother pressed her hand to his father's forehead. She turned to Anik with a worried expression and said, "His fever is still very bad. If it does not break soon, he will die."

"Is there anything we can do, mother?" Anik asked.

She shook her head and told him, "I think not, my son. The shaman said that oil from a seal might help him, but this storm is too dangerous for anyone to go out in. The hunters agreed to bring us some seal oil once the storm has passed, but I fear it will be too late by then."

Thinking about his mother's words, Anik decided to kill a seal and bring its oil back for his father. He quietly pulled on his furs to stay warm and grabbed his father's harpoon. While his mother was busy caring for her sick husband, Anik sneaked out of their igloo to brave the storm. As soon as he stepped outside, frost whipped his face, and he struggled to move against the strong winds. Snow pelted him, clinging to his fur clothing, but he forced himself to take one step after another. His progress was slow, but eventually, he made it to the edge of the frozen sea and headed out onto the ice.

The waters were frozen, allowing Anik to walk across the surface, squinting his eyes to see through the haze of the storm. He knew what to look for; holes in the ice the seals used to breathe. It didn't take long for him to find one, but no seals were in sight. Hours passed as Anik waited to glimpse a seal coming to the surface. The wind kept knocking him over, even when he was resting on his knees. He kept having to brush the snow from his clothes, and his face was so numb he could no longer feel it. Anik understood why the hunters refused to go out in this weather. It was miserable.

Anik came close to giving up and returning home empty-handed. His muscles ached from fighting the wind, and his lungs burned from breathing the freezing cold air. Finally, he spotted movement from his half-shut eyes and tightly gripped his father's harpoon. Although he could barely move his arms, he summoned every last ounce of strength he had to thrust the harpoon through the hole in the ice. There was a shrill whine, and the shadow in the water stopped moving. Anik reached into the hole and hauled the dead seal out.

As fast as he could manage, Anik dragged the seal back across the frozen sea, stumbling again and again from the raging winds. He was exhausted by the time he reached his igloo, but he burst inside and called out to his mother.

"I have brought a seal! Come get the oil from it!"

Anik's mother rushed to her son, a combination of fear, anger, and relief showing on her face.

"My son! What have you done? Did you go out in this storm?"

"Yes, mother," he said. "I could not sit by and do nothing while father suffered. Now you can save him."

She pushed his hood down and kissed the top of his head, saying, "You brave, foolish boy! You could have died out there!"

"But I did not," he replied. "Do not worry about me. Do what you need to help father."

His mother hurried to extract the seal's oil and gave it to her husband. She also cut its meat and made a broth for him to eat, as the shaman had told her the seal had great healing powers. Anik was sound asleep, but when he awoke, he also found some meat and broth waiting for him. His mother insisted he eat it to help him recover from his difficult adventure. He did as she asked, but he was still exhausted and fell back asleep when he had finished.

Anik woke up again the next morning and opened his eyes, looking over at where his father had been resting. There was nobody there and, for a moment, he was terrified that his father had died. However, he felt a hand pat his cheek and looked up to see his father smiling down at him.

"I heard what you did to save my life," his father said. "You are braver than every man in this village. I will never forget how you braved the storm and hunted a seal to help me. You will be a great leader when you are grown, and I will be the first to follow you."

His father was right. Anik became the best hunter in the village, and he became known for his bravery. He earned a reputation for achieving incredible feats, helping save many lives, and keeping the village safe. Eventually, the old chief died without any children to take his place. The villagers got together to pick a new chief, and Anik's father was the first to put forward his son's name. After everything Anik had done for them, the decision was easy, and he was chosen to replace the old chief. Anik's father stayed true to his word, serving as his son's top advisor and loyally following his new chief.

Chapter Round-Up Activity

When you read these Inuit tales, could you picture the scenes and characters in your mind?

Take some time to draw your own version of something you really liked from the stories in this chapter. It can be anything you want; a picture of Sedna, an igloo, a seal, a dog sled, or whatever else you want to draw. You can draw your picture on the next page, or if you're using an e-reader or reading in an e-book format, you can draw your picture in a notebook or drawing pad.

My Picture from the Inuit Tales

Chapter 7: Apache Spirituality: The Sacred Hoop and Life's Journey

The Apache people are Native Americans from multiple tribes that originally lived in the Great Plains Southwest of the United States and the northern part of Mexico. They fought many wars against the Spanish Conquistadors, the Mexican people, and the United States Army. The Apache are a fierce and proud people who resisted attempts to push them out of their lands. From 1875 to 1886, the United States forcibly removed the Apache from their homes and resettled them on reservations in Oklahoma, New Mexico, and Arizona.

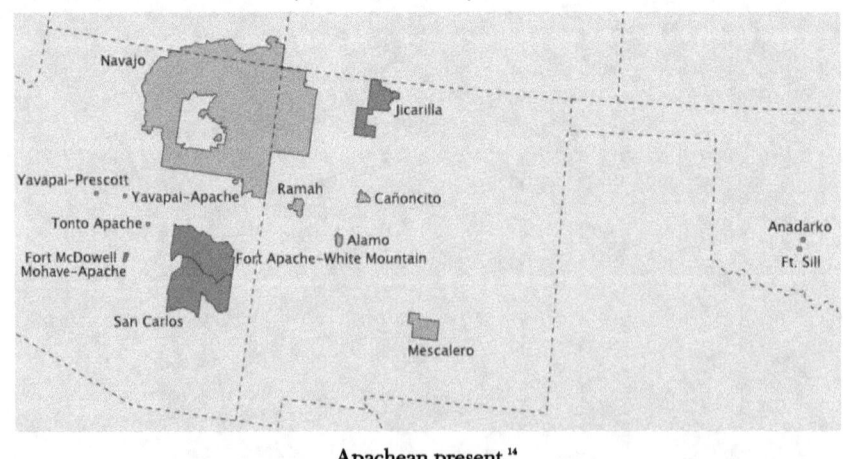

Apachean present.[14]

The Sacred Hoop

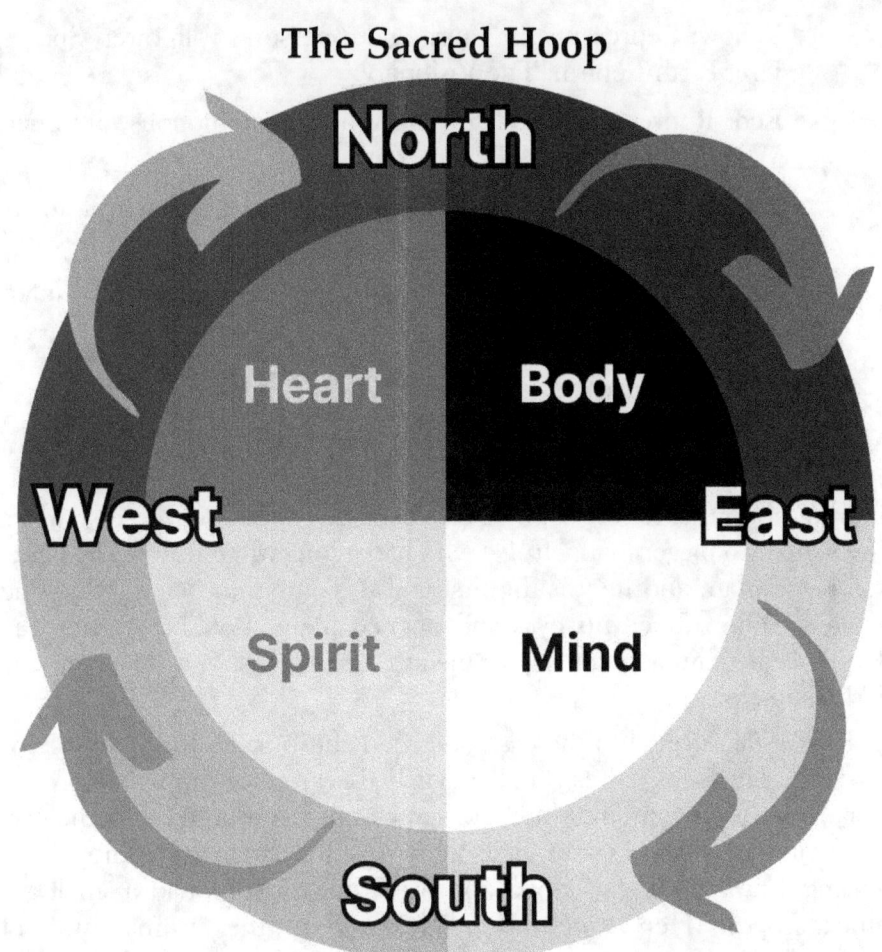

The Sacred Hoop.

The Sacred Hoop is a concept that shows how there is a never-ending cycle to everything in the world. It's divided into four parts, each with a different color: yellow, red, black, and white. The Sacred Hoop is set up so that the points where each quarter of the hoop meets represent a cardinal direction, with north, south, east, and west laid out like on a map or compass. The cycle on the Sacred Hoop flows to the right, and each color represents many different parts of life and the world.

A major part of the Sacred Hoop is that it shows the four aspects of a person: their mind, body, heart, and spirit. It can also show the four seasons, the four elements, the four phases of life, and the four roles of Apache culture. The colors of the Sacred Hoop are matched up with the following parts of each group:

- **Yellow:** Represents the Spirit and a person's willpower, Spring, Fire, Birth/Rebirth, The Visionary.

- **Red:** Represents the Heart and a person's emotions, Summer, Water, Growth, and The Teacher.

- **Black:** Represents the Body and a person's physical form, Autumn, Earth, Maturity, The Healer.

- **White:** Represents the Mind and a person's intellect, Winter, Air, Death, The Warrior.

Apache Creation Myth

At the start of the universe, there was nothing but darkness. Out of nowhere, a small, thin disc appeared. The top side was colored yellow, and the bottom side was colored black. In the middle of the disc was a tiny man – no bigger than a frog – who had a long white beard. His name was Kuterastan, and he was the first god to come into being. When he awakened, he rubbed his eyes and opened them. Looking up into the darkness, he saw a bright light appear. The light shone down on the darkness below.

Kuterastan looked to the east, and the light took on the yellow color of dawn. He looked west, and the light became an amber color like dusk. He searched around him and saw clouds that weren't there before. After rubbing his eyes and face, he shook the sweat from his hands, flinging it away. Another cloud appeared, but this one had a small girl sitting atop it. Her name was Stenatliha – or the "woman without parents." As Kuterastan and Stenatliha looked at each other, they seemed confused.

"Where did you come from?" Kuterastan asked.

"I do not know," Stenatliha answered. "Where did *you* come from?"

"I do not know, either," he replied.

She thought for a moment and then said, "You should come join me on my cloud."

He climbed off the disc and sat down beside her. Once again, he rubbed his eyes and face, shaking his hands and flinging sweat everywhere. The sweat transformed into Chuganaai, or the Sun, and Hadintin Skhin, or Pollen Boy. For a long time, all four of the gods sat on the cloud in complete silence. None of them knew what to say or do.

It was Kuterastan who spoke first, asking, "What shall we do?"

"We could create something," Stenatliha suggested.

Pollen Boy frowned and said, "But what should we create?"

"It does not matter," Chuganaai insisted. "Just make the first thing that comes to mind."

So Kuterastan flicked his sweat and made Nacholecho, the Tarantula. He followed this up by creating the Big Dipper, the Wind, the Lightning, the Thunder, and the Moon. The gods assigned each a task. However, as they sat on the cloud, they agreed that it wasn't a very good home. All four gods dripped beads of sweat into Kuterastan's hands. He closed his palms, and when he opened them again, there was a little brown ball the size of a bean. The four gods kicked the ball back and forth, causing it to grow each time.

The Wind entered the ball and caused it to get even bigger. Nacholecho attached a black cord to the ball and stretched it out far to the east. He then attached a white cord and stretched it to the south, a yellow cord that stretched to the east, and a red cord that stretched to the north. Finally, the gods stuck poles into each cord to hold it in place.

"The world is now made, and it sits still," Kuterastan said and repeated this phrase over and over.

Kuterastan, Stenatliha, and Pollen Boy entered the world to live there. However, Chuganaai chose to remain in the skies above, having fallen in love with the Moon. She did not return his feelings, but he continues to chase her around the world each day, never able to catch up to her. The other three gods used their sweat to form the oceans, mountains, plants, and animals. Finally, Kuterastan and Stenatliha combined their sweat and created the first humans, teaching them all about their new world.

Hauzini's Sunrise Dance Ceremony

Hanuzi's sunrise dance ceremony statue.[16]

The time had arrived for Hauzini's coming-of-age ceremony, which all Apache girls must go through: the Sunrise Dance Ceremony. She wasn't looking forward to it, dreading the fact that she would be spending the next four days doing nothing but dancing in place. She didn't understand why it was so important. Nothing would change just because she bounced around for four days in a row. She begged her mother to let her skip it, but her mother was outraged that she would even ask. It seemed that there was no way for her to get out of participating in the ceremony.

A blanket was set out a little way from their village for Hauzini to stand on and perform the dance. At sundown, the ceremony began. The tribe's medicine man started the ceremony with a blessing, and then she was told to stand on the blanket. Her mother dressed her in buckskins, scarves, beads, shells, and sacred yellow pollen. She was given a curved staff that was to be used to keep in rhythm with the music being played. The last part of her outfit was a large eagle feather placed in her hair. As the drums beat, she danced by shifting her weight from one foot to the other throughout each traditional song.

On the first night, 32 songs were played by the medicine man and a group of chosen singers. Hauzini was tired by the time they were finished and was glad to go to her meditation teepee, which was built specifically for the ceremony. It was set up close to where she danced, and she was meant to spend the night in prayer. She had to fast throughout the ceremony, only being given water to drink. As she meditated and prayed, an owl flew down from the sky and landed in front of her. She stared at it and wondered why it had come. When it opened its beak, instead of hearing a hoot, it actually spoke to her.

"Hello, Changing Woman," the owl said. "I have come to pay my respects."

"I am Hauzini, not the Changing Woman," she replied.

The owl laughed and told her, "I have known you since the beginning, Changing Woman. You cannot fool me."

The owl then flew away, leaving Hauzini confused. At sunrise, she returned to the blanket to dance again. It was hot and humid, which left her uncomfortable dressed in her outfit. After six hours of dancing, people from the village and beyond came to offer her blessings. Others came to be blessed by her because they believed the sacred yellow pollen gave her special healing powers. She touched them and spoke the traditional prayers of healing, and they thanked her, calling her Changing Woman, just like the owl had.

Her tribe feasted that evening, having acorn stew, barbecue corn, beans, and cornbread. She smelled the food and felt her stomach rumbling with hunger, but all she could have was more water. The Crown Dancers arrived and danced with bells to 32 songs. Hauzini danced with them, and they offered blessings from the spirits to her. At midnight, the Crown Dancers finished and left, followed by the rest of the tribe. However, Hauzini had to dance all through the night to the beat of the medicine man's drums.

During the night, a coyote stalked toward her from the darkness. She looked at it fearfully and called out a warning to the medicine man, but he didn't seem to hear her. Hauzini was about to stop dancing so she could run away, but the coyote opened its mouth and spoke.

"Do not be afraid, Changing Woman. I have only come to pay my respects."

"Thank you, Coyote," Hauzini said.

The coyote turned and walked away. Inside, Hauzini began to feel different. Her muscles stopped aching, and her bones felt stronger. By the morning, all weariness had melted away from her body. The sun climbed into the sky, and she stopped dancing so she could mash corn and clay together so the tribe could paint her yellow from head to toe. Another 32 songs were played for the now-painted Hauzini to dance along with. The Crown Dancers returned to join her one more time. Her tribe built an altar in her teepee, laying out sacred feathers on it and offering prayers.

Hauzini continued to dance alone all night, and instead of feeling tired, she felt the power of her ancestors flowing through her. When a bear appeared before her, she smiled at it and greeted it first.

"Hello, my old friend," she said. "It is good to see you again."

"It is good to see you, too, Changing Woman," the bear replied. "I wished to come pay my respects."

"Thank you, old friend," Hauzini replied gratefully. "I appreciate your thoughtfulness."

When the sun rose that morning, her tribe returned to finish the ceremony. Her mother took her down to the river to wash her. The medicine man gave a final blessing and released Hauzini. After carefully removing each item of her outfit, she was allowed to go home and sleep. Now that it was over, she felt exhausted and was happy for the chance to rest. When she awoke the next day, having slept for almost 24 hours, she no longer felt like a girl – she was a changed woman.

Chapter Round-Up Activity

How much have you learned about the Apache people? Can you fill in the blanks to complete these statements? See how well you can do by completing the following sentences:

1. In the Apache creation myth, the first god to come into being was named _____.

2. Apache girls become the _____ _____ during the Sunrise Dance Ceremony.

3. The red part of the Sacred Hoop represents the Heart, summer, _____, Growth, and the Teacher.

4. The Apache were forced onto reservations between the years _____ and _____.

5. Based on Apache legend, the world was created by the _____ of the four original gods of creation.

Answers

1. Kuterastan
2. Changing Woman
3. Water
4. 1875 and 1886
5. Sweat

Chapter 8: The Hopi and the Corn Mother: Tales of Agriculture and Survival

The Hopi people are Native Americans living in the Southwestern United States, mainly in northeastern Arizona. They have a lot in common with the Navajo and the Pueblo peoples, such as living in homes made from adobe and honoring kachina spirits. The Hopi have a female-based culture, with families centered on the women. Children are considered part of their mother's clan, while the women of the father's clan get to name them. The Hopi people are subsistence farmers, so they only grow enough food to feed themselves and their families or communities.

Map of the Hopi Reservation[16]

The Corn Mother

Traditional Hopi Woman.[17]

Many ages before today, food in the lands of the Hopi was hard to come by. Not far from a starving tribe lived an old woman known as the Corn Mother. War or starvation caused children to become orphans, and one of the orphans wandered away from his village, ending up at the Corn Mother's home. Taking pity on the child, she took him into her home. He, too, was starving, and she couldn't bear to watch the boy suffer. In secret, she rubbed her body and produced grains of corn for him to eat. When he returned to his tribe, they couldn't understand how he seemed well-fed while they themselves continued to starve.

One day, a man from the tribe went to visit the Corn Mother. He begged her to help feed his tribe by whatever means she had fed the orphan. She took pity on him, just like the child, and agreed to bring them food. Again, she rubbed her body, filling a large basket with grains of corn. When she brought the food to the tribe, they were overjoyed and finally filled their starving bellies. The tribe's chief thanked the Corn Mother for her generosity and invited her to join them. They gave her a house in the village, and she was happy to be accepted by the people.

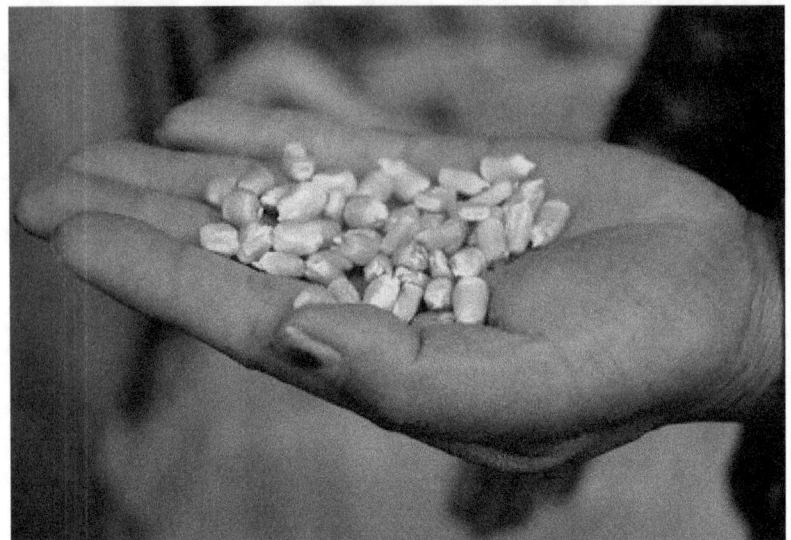

The Corn Mother fed the tribe with the corn she made from her body.[18]

The Corn Mother kept the tribe fed for several years but became weaker every time she made corn from her body. The tribe depended on her to survive, and she feared the time would come when she could no longer feed them. During an unusually cold winter, the tribe once again had no food. Making the corn for everyone took a toll on the Corn Mother, and she became too weak to stand. The chief went to her home, where he found her lying in bed and begged her to give them more food. Since she could not get out of bed to make the corn in secret, she first refused, but the chief pleaded with her on behalf of the starving children.

She took pity on the tribe and told the chief to bring her a basket. When he carried it to her, she rubbed her body to create the grains of corn for them to eat. However, seeing how their food had been made disgusted the chief. He called her a witch and spread the word to the tribe. They decided to burn her for using evil magic to make the corn. Before she was burned, the orphan she first helped tried to convince the tribe not to kill her. They ignored his pleas, but the Corn Mother was grateful to him for trying.

The orphan hugged the Corn Mother with tears, apologizing for failing to help her the way she helped him. She told him not to cry and instructed him to bury her bones in a field after she was dead. The tribe dragged the Corn Mother far from their village and set her on fire, leaving her to burn to death. They then returned to their homes, but the orphan stayed behind, begging the spirits to prevent the Corn Mother from suffering and asking them to take care of her when she joined them.

After the flames died out, the orphan collected her bones and found an empty field in which to bury her bones. He returned to his village, saddened at the loss of the kind old woman who saved him and his tribe. Every day, the orphan went to the Corn Mother's grave to offer a blessing and honor her sacrifice. He noticed that plants were starting to sprout all across the field. Great big stalks rose up throughout the summer, each one holding husks of corn. By the end of the summer, huge ears of corn were ripe to be picked.

Despite their poor treatment of the Corn Mother, she had provided the tribe with a way to keep the starving people fed. They ate the corn, but the orphan saved some to remove the kernels and plant them in the field. In this way, the tribe was able to grow corn crops every year and feed themselves well. The gift given to them by the Corn Mother was shared with others in the area, allowing them all to survive. When the orphan grew up and had a family of his own, he made sure to pass on the story of the Corn Mother to his children. Many years later, he died with a full belly and a loving family surrounding him, and his spirit was finally reunited with the Corn Mother.

Chapter Round-Up Activity

Do you like to eat corn? Have you ever seen a cornfield? Would you like to watch it grow? You can plant your own corn to see how it goes from a seed to a cornstalk that produces big ears of corn. All you have to do is follow these instructions to make your own corn to pick and enjoy:

What You Need:

- A plant pot
- Potting mix soil
- Fertilizer
- Watering can
- Corn seeds (kernels)

Directions:

1. Fill the pot with your potting mix soil until it's about 2 inches from the top.
2. Dig a small hole in the center of the soil about 1 to 2 inches deep.
3. Drop in your corn seeds and cover them back up with the soil.
4. Use the watering can to pour plenty of water into the pot.
5. Spread some fertilizer over the soil.
6. Place the pot in a spot where it can get 6 to 8 hours of sunlight daily.
7. Make sure you keep the soil moist and use the fertilizer on it once every 14 days.
8. Within two to three months, you will have your own corn!

Chapter 9: Tlingit Totems: Carving Histories and Clan Legends

The Tlingit people are Native Americans who live in Alaska and the Pacific Northwest Coast of the United States. They have a system of kinship or family structure based on the female line. As with the Hopi, children are considered part of their mother's clan, and roles and property are passed down from mother to daughter. A big part of Tlingit life revolves around catching and eating salmon, but they also hunt land and sea mammals.

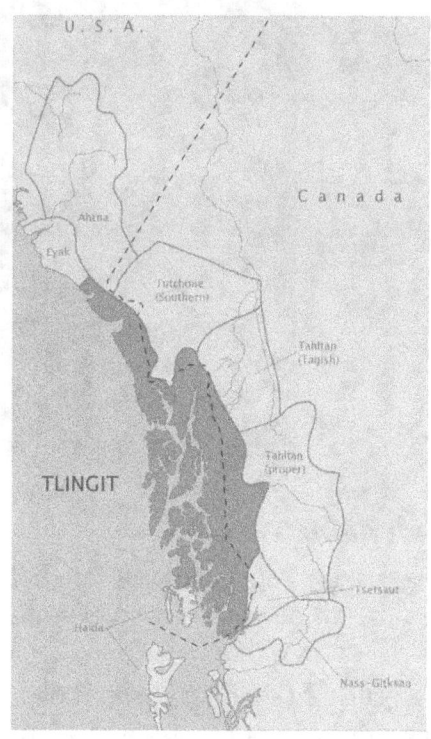

The map of Tinglit.[19]

Totem Poles

One major aspect of Tlingit culture is the carefully crafted and highly detailed totem poles they create. These totem poles are usually made from cedar trees, and the figures they carve tell a story. Many totem poles use animals to represent different ideas, traditions, or folktales, allowing them to express their own unique version of events for people to see. Observers need to be familiar with the legends and mythology of Tlingit culture to understand what the totem poles mean.

A Tinglit totem pole.[30]

Types of Totem Poles

Lineage Pole (Entrance Pole): These are often used as support rafters on the inside and outside of houses. They show a family's history and social status within their tribe.

Native Legend and Story Pole: These display figures to represent the legends and stories passed down through the generations of the tribe.

Memorial Pole: These are carved to honor the lives of important elders and tribe members, especially those who have done great deeds or aided the tribe in some way.

Commemorative Pole: These are made to mark major celebrations, festivals, feasts, and other special events.

Grave Marker Pole: These are carved with figures to represent the lives of dead tribe members. They are hollowed out in order to hold the remains of the dead.

Common Totem Pole Figures

The Thunderbird is a common totem.[31]

Raven: The Raven is a major figure in many Tlingit legends. He is a trickster spirit who uses his wits and intelligence to defeat greedy or evil individuals and help the good people they hurt. There are groups of Tlingit clans who use the Raven as their symbol.

Thunderbird: The Thunderbird is believed to flap its wings and create the thunder heard during thunderstorms. One legend tells of how the Thunderbird helped the Tlingit when the Whale ate all the sea fish. The Thunderbird used its mighty wings to battle the Whale, defeating it and allowing the Tlingit to catch fish once again.

Eagle: The Eagle represents the wind and the skies. It is considered a sacred animal, and its feathers are said to hold great power. Like the Raven, groups of clans have taken the Eagle as their symbol.

Otter: The Otter is another major figure in Tlingit mythology. A group of helpful shapeshifting spirits known as the *Kushtaka* often appear in the form of the Otter. They can also transform into a half-human and half-otter being. The Kushtaka aid the Tlingit by giving them food and guidance.

Wolf: The Wolf is one of the few land animals that appear in Tlingit legends. It represents a combination of danger, strength, and hunting skills. As with the Raven and the Eagle, groups of clans use the Wolf as their symbol.

The Raven and the Box of Light

The Raven.

A man called Nass Shaak Aankáawu, or the "Nobleman at the Head of the Nass River," was greedy. He collected many treasures, keeping them all to himself. His most precious treasures were every form of light, which he kept in boxes stored in his home. This left the world covered in never-ending darkness. The people begged Nass Shaak Aankáawu to return the light so they could have a day and a night, but he refused. He didn't want to share his treasures with anyone else because he believed he deserved to have everything he desired.

There was a trickster spirit in the form of a white Raven named Yéil who wanted to know what it was like to be human. While watching the Tlingit people, he saw Nass Shaak Aankáawu's daughter go down to a stream and drink its water every morning. Yéil transformed into a needle from a spruce tree and jumped into the stream. He floated into her cup, and she swallowed him when she drank from it. The woman became pregnant and gave birth to Yéil in human form. Nass Shaak Aankáawu and his daughter adored the child, loving him more than anything else in their lives.

Nass Shaak Aankáawu spoiled his grandson, giving him every toy and luxury the boy could ever want. When the child cried that he wanted the boxes holding the stars, the moon, and the sun, his grandfather could not say no to him. Every time baby Yéil cried for one of the treasures, Nass Shaak Aankáawu gave it to him. As soon as Yéil got the boxes, he opened them up, releasing the stars, the moon, and the sun, returning the light to the world. Nass Shaak Aankáawu was upset at losing his treasures, but the people and animals were delighted to have them back.

Realizing he had been tricked, Nass Shaak Aankáawu wanted revenge for losing his treasures. He grabbed Yéil and held him over the fireplace, letting him become marked by the smoke. Yéil's human form melted away, and he was once again in the shape of a Raven. The smoke changed his coloring from white to black; from that day on, every raven would be born with feathers the color of coal. The Tlingit people honored Yéil by carving the Raven at the top of their totem poles, thanking him for returning the light to them.

Chapter Round-Up Activity

Do you have a story you want to tell? Maybe there's someone important in your life you want to honor. You can create a totem pole to express whatever you want. To make one yourself, here's what you need to do:

What You Need:

- Drawing paper
- Paper towel tube
- Crayons or markers
- Scissors
- Tape
- Ruler

Directions:

1. Use the crayons or markers to draw figures of animals or symbols. Make 3 or 4 figures about 3 inches tall and 2 to 3 inches wide. Measure your drawings with the ruler to make sure they're the right size.

2. Cut out the figures you drew with the scissors.

3. Make a loop with the tape so the sticky side is on the outside and stick it to the back of each cutout figure.

4. Attach the cutout figures with the tape to the paper towel tube. Place them one on top of the other, making them look like a totem pole. The tube is 11 inches tall, so they should all fit if you measured your figures correctly. Part of the top figure can be a bit above the top of the tube.

Display your totem pole where people can see it. Explain to them the story you've created and what each figure represents.

Conclusion

It's good to get into the habit of expanding your mind by learning new things. There are people worldwide who live in a way completely different from your own. When you take the time to explore their history and culture, you will find that there's more than one way to do things. Some people have ideas, traditions, and beliefs that aren't the same as yours, but it doesn't mean you can't understand why they live the way they do.

The Native Americans have done their best to keep their culture and spirit alive. Being pushed out of their homelands and onto reservations also came with the United States trying to make them change. There have been many attempts to force the Native American tribes into becoming more like the people of the United States, as well as trying to convert them from their traditional religions to Christianity. This has left the Native Americans struggling to balance their original culture with the culture of the rest of the country.

Now that you've learned many new things about the different Native American tribes, you can help them keep their culture alive. Spread these tales by telling them to your family and friends. Show them the projects you've made that are based on Native American arts and crafts. Talk about the facts you discovered – since many people never learned them in school. Think about everything you read and how you can use the lessons taught by these Native American stories in your own daily life.

Check out another book in the series

Welcome Aboard, Check Out This Limited-Time Free Bonus!

Ahoy, reader! Welcome to the Ahoy Publications family, and thanks for snagging a copy of this book! Since you've chosen to join us on this journey, we'd like to offer you something special.

Check out the link below for a FREE e-book filled with delightful facts about American History.

But that's not all - you'll also have access to our exclusive email list with even more free e-books and insider knowledge. Well, what are ye waiting for? Click the link below to join and set sail toward exciting adventures in American History.

Access your bonus here

https://ahoypublications.com/

Or, Scan the QR code!

References

Access Genealogy. (2011, July 9). Blackfoot Tribe | Access Genealogy. Access Genealogy.
http://www.accessgenealogy.com/native/tribes/siouan/blackfoothist.htm

All Tribes. (2019). Types of Native American Kachina Dolls. Alltribes.com.
https://alltribes.com/types-of-native-american-kachina-dolls/

Arizona Museum of Natural History. (2020, October 22). Apache Sunrise Dance and Ceremony | Arizona Museum of Natural History. Www.arizonamuseumofnaturalhistory.org.
https://www.arizonamuseumofnaturalhistory.org/explore-the-museum/exhibitions/athapascan-way/apache-sunrise-dance-and-ceremony#ad-image-0

Associated Press. (1962, March 25). Article on Bob Barker 1962. Argus-Leader, 17. https://www.newspapers.com/article/argus-leader-article-on-bob-barker-1962/93129234/

Belarde-Lewis, M. (2019, July 21). There are many versions of the Tlingit "Raven" story, but its truth and hopeful message are universal. The Seattle Times. https://www.seattletimes.com/pacific-nw-magazine/there-are-many-versions-of-the-tlingit-raven-story-but-its-truth-and-hopeful-message-are-universal/

Borré, K. (1994). The Healing Power of the Seal: The Meaning of Intuit Health Practice and Belief. Arctic Anthropology, 31(1), 1–15. https://www.jstor.org/stable/40316345

Brummett, Jr., R. (1982). The Tribes and the States. Www.sidis.net. https://www.sidis.net/TSContents.htm

Corn Mothers. (2016). Corn Mothers | Home. Www.cornmothers.com. https://www.cornmothers.com/

Drexler, K. (2019, January 22). Research Guides: Indian Removal Act: Primary Documents in American History: Introduction. Loc.gov; Library of Congress. https://guides.loc.gov/indian-removal-act

Farrand, T. (2022, August 3). Corn Mother: Mythical origins of the world's most produced crop. Www.artsundivided.com. https://www.artsundivided.com/post/2022-08-03-corn-mother

Goseyun, A. E. (2023). Balch Institute—Rites of Passage—Sunrise Ceremonial. Hsp.org. https://www2.hsp.org/exhibits/Balch%20exhibits/rites/apache.html

Grossnickle Hines, A. (2016, March 4). Peaceful Pieces. Web.archive.org. https://web.archive.org/web/20160304033735/http://www.aghines.com/anna_html_pages/peaceful/peacemaker.htm

Johnson, E. (2019). Sutori. Www.sutori.com. https://www.sutori.com/en/story/dekanawida-the-great-peacemaker--XGmBGZdZKqmxjVz5kjEEPjpE

Kachina House. (2021, March 23). 10 Navajo Symbols and Their Meanings. Kachina House's Blog. https://blog.kachinahouse.com/10-important-navajo-symbols-and-their-meanings/

Klein, C. (2019, November 7). How Native Americans Struggled to Survive on the Trail of Tears. History.com. https://www.history.com/news/trail-of-tears-conditions-cherokee

Kudu, R. (2016, October 16). Rain Dance of Zuni. Www.inquiry.net. http://www.inquiry.net/outdoor/native/dance/rain_zuni.htm

Library of Congress. (2011). New Mexico. The Rain Dance. Zuni Pueblo. Library of Congress, Washington, D.C. 20540 USA. https://www.loc.gov/item/2017657465/

Mescalero Apache Tribe. (2019). Our Culture. Mescaleroapachetribe.com. https://mescaleroapachetribe.com/our-culture/

Minges, P. (1994). Beneath the Underdog: Race, Religion and the Trail of Tears. Cherokee, Native American. U.S. Data Repository, USGenNet Inc. Www.us-Data.org. https://www.us-data.org/us/minges/underdog.html

National Park Service. (2016). Bison Bellows: Indigenous Hunting Practices (U.S. National Park Service). Nps.gov. https://www.nps.gov/articles/bison-bellows-3-31-16.htm

Native Languages. (1998). Native Lore: Apache Creation Story. Www.ilhawaii.net. http://www.ilhawaii.net/~stony/lore34.html

Parker, A. C. (1916). ᴧᴧ/ork State Museum Bullet iUl. https://ia801604.us.archive.org/19/items/constitutionoffi00parkuoft/constitutionoffi00parkuoft.pdf

Pembroke, H. (2021, May 21). The History and Significance of Totem Poles. Alaska Wildlife Alliance (AWA). https://www.akwildlife.org/news/the-history-and-significance-of-totem-poles

Roediger, V. M. (1991). Ceremonial Costumes of the Pueblo Indians. Publishing.cdlib.org. https://publishing.cdlib.org/ucpressebooks/view?docId=ft8870087s&chunk.id=d0e1214&toc.depth=1&toc.id=d0e950&brand=ucpress

Severo, R. (2023, August 26). Bob Barker, Longtime Host of "The Price Is Right," Dies at 99. The New York Times. https://www.nytimes.com/2023/08/26/arts/television/bob-barker-dead.html

Soulek, L. (2024, January 12). Native American Treaty Law 101. KELOLAND.com. https://www.keloland.com/news/local-news/native-american-treaty-law-101/

Weiser-Alexander, K. (2018, October). The Thunderbird of Native Americans – Legends of America. Www.legendsofamerica.com. https://www.legendsofamerica.com/thunderbird-native-american/

Image Sources

1 https://commons.wikimedia.org/wiki/File:Navajo_flag.svg

2 https://commons.wikimedia.org/wiki/File:Navajo_winter_hogan.jpg

3 By Noahedits, CC BY-SA 4.0 <https://creativecommons.org/licenses/by-sa/4.0>, via Wikimedia Commons: https://commons.wikimedia.org/wiki/File:Lakota_map.svg:

4 https://commons.wikimedia.org/wiki/File:En-chief-sitting-bull.jpg

5 https://commons.wikimedia.org/wiki/File:Young-Man-Afraid-of-His-Horses_(Tashun-Kakokipa),_an_Oglala_Sioux,_standing_in_front_of_his_lodge,_Pine_Ridge,_South_Dak_-_NARA_-_530813.jpg

6 By Original Compiled by Aaron Walden. Vector derivative by Jdcollins13, CC BY-SA 3.0 <https://creativecommons.org/licenses/by-sa/3.0>, via Wikimedia Commons: https://commons.wikimedia.org/wiki/File:Great_seal_of_the_cherokee_nation.svg

7 https://commons.wikimedia.org/w/index.php?curid=334447

8 https://commons.wikimedia.org/w/index.php?curid=997266

9 https://commons.wikimedia.org/w/index.php?curid=6735601

10 By Junuxx at Dutch Wikipedia, CC BY-SA 3.0, https://commons.wikimedia.org/w/index.php?curid=1809070

11 Ansgar Walk, CC BY-SA 3.0 <http://creativecommons.org/licenses/by-sa/3.0/>, via Wikimedia Commons https://commons.wikimedia.org/w/index.php?curid=838934

12 Sailko, CC BY 3.0 <https://creativecommons.org/licenses/by/3.0>, via Wikimedia Commons: https://commons.wikimedia.org/wiki/File:Canada,_qaqaq_ashoona,_sedna,_madre_dei_mari,_legno,_1988,JPG

13 https://commons.wikimedia.org/wiki/File:Inupiat_Family_from_Noatak,_Alaska,_1929,_Edward_S._Curtis_(restored).jpg

14 By Ish ishwar (talk · contribs), CC BY-SA 3.0 <http://creativecommons.org/licenses/by-sa/3.0/>, via Wikimedia Commons: https://commons.wikimedia.org/wiki/File:Apachean_present.png:

15 By Kimi Eisele: https://borderlore.org/my-sunrise/: https://borderlore.org/wp-content/gallery/apache-sunrise-ceremony/21-CornPollen.jpg

16 Hopi flag by Mario1952Navajo flag map is my own work, CC BY-SA 4.0 <https://creativecommons.org/licenses/by-sa/4.0>, via Wikimedia Commons https://commons.wikimedia.org/wiki/File:Flag_map_of_the_Hopi_Reservation.png

17 https://commons.wikimedia.org/wiki/File:Hopi_woman_with_a_traditional_pot_and_traditional_clothing.png

18 Cimmyt, Attribution-NonCommercial-ShareAlike 2.0 Generic, BY-NC-SA 2.0 < https://creativecommons.org/licenses/by-nc-sa/2.0/deed.en> https://www.flickr.com/photos/cimmyt/5758809079

19 By Goddard (1996, 1999): https://commons.wikimedia.org/wiki/File:Tlingit-map.png

20 Mharrsch, Attribution-NonCommercial-ShareAlike 2.0 Generic, CC BY-NC-SA 2.0 < https://creativecommons.org/licenses/by-nc-sa/2.0/deed.en> https://www.flickr.com/photos/mharrsch/523470396

21 Pahphotos, Attribution-NonCommercial-NoDerivs 2.0 Generic, CC BY-NC-ND 2.0 <https://creativecommons.org/licenses/by-nc-nd/2.0/deed.en> https://www.flickr.com/photos/pahphotos/3620645429

www.ingramcontent.com/pod-product-compliance
Lightning Source LLC
Chambersburg PA
CBHW071538120626
46550CB00006B/2498